ALGORITHMIC TRADING 101

A Practical Introduction to Automated Market Trading for Non-Programmers

Usiere Uko

Copyright © 2024 Usiere Uko

All Rrghts reserved.

No part of this publication may be reproduced, distributed, or transmitted in any form or by any means, including photocopying, recording, or other electronic or mechanical methods, without the prior written permission of the publisher, except in the case of brief quotations embodied in critical reviews and certain other noncommercial uses permitted by copyright law.
This publication is designed to provide accurate and authoritative information in regard to the subject matter covered. It is sold with the understanding that the publisher is not engaged in rendering legal, accounting, or other professional services. If legal advice or other expert assistance is required, the services of a competent professional should be sought.
The author and publisher shall not be liable for any loss of profit or any other commercial damages, including but not limited to special, incidental, consequential, or other damages.

ISBN-13: 979-8-332-14542-1

FIRST EDITION

CONTENTS

Title Page
Copyright
INTRODUCTION
PART: 1: INTRODUCTION TO ALGORITHMIC TRADING   1
Chapter 2: Benefits and Risks of Algorithmic Trading   2
Chapter 3: Overview of how algorithms automate trading decisions   6
Chapter 1: What is algorithmic trading?   10
PART: 2: GETTING STARTED WITH ALGORITHMIC TRADING   17
Chapter 4: Understanding basic trading concepts   18
Chapter 5: Choosing a trading platform or service that supports algorithmic trading   25
Chapter 6: Setting up an account and accessing market data   29
Chapter 7: How to Install and Use Expert Advisors (EA) on MetaTrader4   33
PART: 3: EXPLORING SIMPLE TRADING STRATEGIES   37
Chapter 8: Introduction to basic trading strategies   38
Chapter 9: Strategy templates or pre-configured strategies   48
Chapter 10: How to select a strategy that aligns with your risk tolerance and investment goals   53
PART: 4: USING TRADING SIGNALS AND INDICATORS   61

Chapter 11: Understanding trading signals and technical indicators — 62

Chapter 12: How to interpret signals and use them in decision-making — 72

Chapter 13: Incorporating signals into your trading strategy — 80

PART: 5: BACKTESTING YOUR STRATEGIES — 85

Chapter 14: Importance of Backtesting to Evaluate Strategy Performance — 86

Chapter 15: Tools and platforms that offer backtesting functionalities — 92

Chapter 16: Interpreting backtest results and refining strategies based on findings — 98

PART: 6: MANAGING RISK IN ALGORITHMIC TRADING — 105

Chapter 17: Risk management principles — 106

Chapter 18: Setting up stop-loss orders and other risk control measures — 112

Chapter 19: Strategies for diversification and portfolio management — 117

PART: 7: DEPLOYING AND MONITORING ALGORITHMS — 121

Chapter 20: How to deploy your algorithmic strategies in live markets — 122

Chapter 21: Tips for monitoring performance and making adjustments — 127

Chapter 22: Understanding transaction costs and their impact on profitability. — 133

PART: 8: PRACTICAL CONSIDERATIONS AND PITFALLS — 139

Chapter 23: Common challenges faced by non-programmers in algorithmic trading. — 140

Chapter 24: Technology and Infrastructure Requirements — 145

Chapter 25: Strategies for dealing with market volatility — 151

and unexpected events.
Chapter 26: Resources and further reading	156
Conclusion and next steps	161
About The Author	165
Books In This Series	167
Books By This Author	169

INTRODUCTION

A PRACTICAL INTRODUCTION TO AUTOMATED MARKET TRADING FOR NON-PROGRAMMERS

Welcome to Algorithmic Trading 101: A Practical Introduction to Automated Market Trading for Non-Programmers. In today's financial landscape, algorithmic trading has revolutionized how markets operate, offering individuals and institutions alike the ability to execute trades with speed, precision, and efficiency.

This book is designed specifically for those interested in harnessing the power of algorithmic trading without needing extensive programming skills.

Why This Book?

Algorithmic trading, once reserved for quantitative analysts and programmers, is now accessible to a broader audience. Whether you're a novice investor or a seasoned trader looking to automate strategies, this book provides a comprehensive yet accessible guide to understanding and implementing algorithmic trading techniques.

What You Will Learn

Throughout this book, we will cover:

Fundamentals of Algorithmic Trading: From defining algorithmic trading to exploring its benefits and risks.

Practical Applications: Techniques for implementing automated trading strategies without programming.

Tools and Platforms: How to select and utilize algorithmic trading platforms and services.

Advanced Topics: Introduction to machine learning applications in trading and regulatory considerations.

Resources for Further Learning: A curated list of resources to deepen your knowledge and skills in automated trading.

Who Should Read This Book?

This book is ideal for non-programmers who already have some basic knowledge and experience in trading and are eager to explore algorithmic trading. If you want to gain practical insights into automated market strategies and navigate the complexities of modern financial markets, this book is for you.

Whether you're a trader, investor, or financial enthusiast with a foundational understanding of trading principles, this practical introduction will equip you with the tools and knowledge to embark on your algorithmic trading journey effectively.

Get ready to embark on a journey into the exciting world of algorithmic trading. By the end of this book, you'll have the confidence and understanding to implement automated trading strategies, optimize trading decisions, and navigate the evolving landscape of automated market trading.

PART: 1: INTRODUCTION TO ALGORITHMIC TRADING

CHAPTER 2: BENEFITS AND RISKS OF ALGORITHMIC TRADING

Algorithmic trading offers both significant benefits and inherent risks for non-programmers looking to participate in financial markets using automated strategies. This chapter examines the advantages and potential pitfalls of algorithmic trading, providing insights to help non-programmers make informed decisions and maximize the benefits while managing the risks effectively.

BENEFITS OF ALGORITHMIC TRADING

1. Accessibility and Ease of Use

One of the primary benefits of algorithmic trading for non-programmers is its accessibility and ease of use. Trading platforms and software have evolved to offer intuitive interfaces and user-friendly tools that simplify the process of creating and deploying automated trading strategies. You can leverage these platforms to implement complex trading algorithms without needing to write code or understand programming languages deeply.

2. Elimination of Emotional Bias

Emotional bias is a common challenge in manual trading,

where decisions may be influenced by fear, greed, or other human emotions. Algorithmic trading reduces these biases by executing trades based on predefined rules and parameters. This approach helps you to maintain discipline and consistency in your trading strategies, leading to more objective decision-making and potentially better trading outcomes.

3. Speed and Efficiency

Algorithmic trading algorithms can analyze market data and execute trades at speeds far beyond human capabilities. For traders, this speed and efficiency are crucial advantages, allowing them to capitalize on fleeting market opportunities, execute trades promptly, and react swiftly to changing market conditions without manual intervention.

4. Precision and Automation

By automating trading decisions, algorithmic trading ensures precision in trade execution and adherence to predetermined strategies. You can set specific criteria for entry and exit points, risk management, and position sizing, which are executed automatically by the algorithm. This automation reduces the likelihood of manual errors and enhances overall trading efficiency.

5. Backtesting and Optimization

Algorithmic trading platforms often include robust backtesting functionalities that allow users to test trading strategies against historical market data. You can utilize these tools to evaluate the performance of your strategies, identify strengths and weaknesses, and make data-driven optimizations. This capability empowers you to refine your approaches without risking capital in real-time markets.

6. Diversification and Portfolio Management

For traders managing diversified investment portfolios, algorithmic trading offers tools to manage multiple strategies across different asset classes and markets simultaneously. Automated trading systems can monitor and rebalance portfolios based on predefined rules, ensuring that investment objectives and risk profiles are maintained effectively over time.

7. Scalability and Customization

Algorithmic trading strategies can be scaled up or down easily to accommodate changing market conditions or investment goals. You can customize your strategies to incorporate specific preferences, market insights, or risk management techniques without needing advanced programming skills. This flexibility enables you to adapt quickly to evolving market dynamics.

RISKS OF ALGORITHMIC TRADING

1. Technical Failures:

Technical failures, such as connectivity issues or software glitches, can lead to missed opportunities or erroneous trades. Traders should ensure robust system monitoring and backup plans to minimize disruptions.

2. Market Uncertainty:

Algorithms may struggle to adapt to unforeseen market conditions or extreme volatility, leading to unexpected losses. Traders should regularly monitor and adjust algorithms based on market dynamics and risk factors.

3. Over-Reliance on Automation:

Depending too heavily on automated trading can reduce oversight and control over investment decisions. You should maintain a balanced approach, supplementing automated strategies with manual monitoring and intervention when necessary.

4. Complexity and Learning Curve:

Developing and managing algorithmic strategies can be complex, requiring ongoing learning and adaptation. Non-programmers should invest time in understanding basic algorithmic concepts and seek educational resources or expert guidance as needed.

Algorithmic trading provides online traders with a powerful toolset to participate in financial markets competitively and efficiently.

By leveraging automation, eliminating emotional bias, and capitalizing on speed and precision, non-programmers can enhance their trading outcomes and achieve their investment objectives more effectively than through manual trading alone.

CHAPTER 3: OVERVIEW OF HOW ALGORITHMS AUTOMATE TRADING DECISIONS

In this chapter, we explore how algorithms automate trading decisions, providing a comprehensive overview of the process and mechanisms behind algorithmic trading. Understanding this foundational aspect is crucial for non-programmers seeking to harness the power of automated strategies in financial markets.

COMPONENTS OF ALGORITHMIC TRADING ALGORITHMS

Algorithmic trading relies on several key components to function effectively. These components work together to analyze market data, implement trading strategies, and execute trades with precision and speed. Here's an in-depth look at the essential components of algorithmic trading algorithms:

1. DATA ANALYSIS AND PROCESSING

Market Data Collection:

Algorithms gather and process vast amounts of market data, including real-time price movements, trading volumes, and other relevant metrics. This data forms the basis for making informed trading decisions.

Data sources can include stock exchanges, market data

providers, and financial news feeds. High-quality, low-latency data is crucial for the accuracy and performance of algorithmic trading systems.

Historical Data Analysis:

Advanced algorithms often incorporate historical data to identify patterns, trends, and correlations that can inform future trading decisions. Analyzing historical data helps in developing and backtesting trading strategies.

Techniques such as time series analysis, statistical analysis, and machine learning models are employed to gain insights from historical data. These techniques help in predicting future market trends and making data-driven decisions.

Machine Learning Models:

Some algorithms leverage machine learning models to enhance data analysis and prediction capabilities. These models can identify complex patterns and relationships within the data that might be missed by traditional statistical methods.

Common machine learning techniques include supervised learning (e.g., regression, classification), unsupervised learning (e.g., clustering, anomaly detection), and reinforcement learning (e.g., optimizing trading strategies based on feedback from the market).

2. TRADING STRATEGIES AND RULES

Implementation of Strategies:

Algorithms implement predefined trading strategies or rules, which dictate how trades should be executed based on specific market conditions. These strategies can vary widely, depending on the trader's objectives and risk tolerance.

Common strategies include trend following (buying when prices are rising, selling when they are falling), mean reversion (trading based on the assumption that prices will revert to their historical mean), arbitrage (exploiting price discrepancies between different markets), and quantitative models (using mathematical and statistical techniques to identify trading opportunities).

Strategy Complexity:

Trading strategies can range from simple rules, such as moving average crossovers, to highly complex quantitative models that involve multiple variables and sophisticated calculations.

The complexity of a strategy often correlates with the trader's risk tolerance and investment goals. Simple strategies may be easier to implement and understand, while complex strategies may offer higher potential returns but require more advanced skills and technology.

Risk Management:

Effective trading strategies incorporate risk management rules to protect against significant losses. These rules may include setting stop-loss limits, diversifying the portfolio, and adjusting the strategy based on changing market conditions.

Algorithms can also use position sizing techniques to determine the optimal amount of capital to allocate to each trade, balancing the potential rewards against the associated risks.

3. Order Generation and Execution

Trading Signal Generation:

Based on the analyzed data and implemented trading strategies, algorithms generate precise trading signals that indicate when to enter or exit a trade. These signals are derived from the predefined rules and conditions set by the trading strategy.

For example, a trend-following algorithm might generate a buy signal when the price of a stock crosses above its 50-day moving average, and a sell signal when it crosses below.

Order Placement:

Algorithms determine the optimal entry and exit points for trades, taking into account factors such as price, volume, and market conditions. They also decide the type and size of orders to place, such as market orders, limit orders, or stop orders.

Orders are placed automatically by the algorithm, often within milliseconds, to capitalize on market opportunities. This high-speed execution helps traders to take advantage of even the smallest price movements.

Execution Speed and Efficiency:

The speed at which orders are executed is crucial in algorithmic trading, especially for strategies that rely on high-frequency trading or arbitrage. Algorithms are designed to minimize latency and execute orders with maximum efficiency.

Execution algorithms may also include smart order routing (SOR) capabilities, which direct orders to the best available market or exchange to achieve the best possible price and execution quality.

REAL-TIME DECISION-MAKING

Algorithms operate in real-time, continuously monitoring market conditions and adjusting strategies accordingly.

This capability allows for rapid decision-making and adaptation to changing market dynamics, optimizing trading performance.

Understanding how algorithms automate trading decisions is essential for non-programmers looking to leverage automated strategies effectively.

CHAPTER 1: WHAT IS ALGORITHMIC TRADING?

Algorithmic trading, also known as algo trading or automated trading, refers to the use of computer algorithms to execute trading orders in financial markets. These algorithms are designed to follow a set of predefined instructions or rules for placing trades, with the goal of achieving optimal execution and maximizing profit opportunities.

By leveraging computational power and advanced statistical techniques, algo trading aims to enhance trading efficiency, minimize costs, and capitalize on market opportunities that would be difficult or impossible for human traders to identify and exploit in real-time.

UNDERSTANDING ALGORITHMIC TRADING

In traditional trading, decisions to buy or sell securities are typically made by human traders based on analysis of market information, economic indicators, and other factors. Algorithmic trading automates this process by leveraging computer programs that can analyze market data, identify trading opportunities, and execute trades without human intervention.

At its core, algorithmic trading involves the use of pre-programmed instructions to execute trades based on various market conditions. These instructions can be as simple as moving average crossovers or as complex as machine learning models predicting price movements. Key concepts in algorithmic trading include:

Algorithms: Step-by-step procedures or formulas for solving problems. In the context of trading, these algorithms are designed to make trading decisions based on predefined criteria.

Automation: The use of technology to perform tasks with minimal human intervention. In algorithmic trading, automation allows for the execution of trades at speeds and frequencies that would be impossible for a human trader to match.

Backtesting: The process of testing a trading strategy on historical data to evaluate its effectiveness. Backtesting helps traders understand how a strategy would have performed in the past, providing insights into its potential future performance.

Execution: The act of carrying out a trade in the market. In algorithmic trading, execution is handled automatically by the algorithm, ensuring that trades are executed at the optimal time based on the predefined strategy.

HOW ALGORITHMIC TRADING WORKS

Algorithmic trading works by integrating multiple components to create a seamless trading process. Here's a simplified flow of how it operates:

Strategy Development: Traders or developers design trading strategies based on technical indicators, statistical models, or other criteria. These strategies are then encoded into algorithms.

Data Input: The algorithm receives input data, such as historical prices, real-time market data, and news feeds.

Signal Generation: Based on the input data, the algorithm generates trading signals that indicate when to buy or sell an asset.

Order Execution: Once a signal is generated, the algorithm automatically places buy or sell orders in the market.

Monitoring and Adjustment: The algorithm continuously monitors the market and adjusts its trading strategy as necessary, adapting to changing market conditions.

TYPES OF ALGORITHMIC TRADING STRATEGIES

There are various types of algorithmic trading strategies, each with its unique approach and objectives. Understanding these strategies can help traders select the most appropriate one based on their trading style, risk tolerance, and market conditions. Here are some of the most common algorithmic trading strategies:

Trend Following

Trend following strategies involve tracking the direction of market trends and making trades that align with these trends. The basic premise is to buy when prices are rising (uptrend) and sell when prices are falling (downtrend).

Common techniques used in trend following include moving averages, momentum indicators, and trend lines. Moving averages, such as the Simple Moving Average (SMA) or Exponential Moving Average (EMA), help identify the direction of the trend. Momentum indicators, like the Relative Strength Index (RSI) and Moving Average Convergence Divergence (MACD), provide insights into the strength and potential reversals of trends.

Arbitrage

Arbitrage strategies aim to exploit price discrepancies between different markets or instruments to achieve risk-free profits. These opportunities are typically short-lived and require rapid execution.

Examples include spatial arbitrage, where a trader buys an asset in one market and simultaneously sells it in another market where the price is higher, and temporal arbitrage, which exploits price differences over time within the same market.

Market Making

Market making involves providing liquidity to the market by continuously placing buy and sell orders for a particular asset. Market makers profit from the bid-ask spread, the difference between the price at which they buy and the price at which they sell.

Market makers use strategies that involve constantly adjusting their buy and sell prices to match the current market conditions, ensuring they can profit from the spread while maintaining liquidity.

Statistical Arbitrage

Statistical arbitrage relies on quantitative models to identify and exploit market inefficiencies. These strategies often involve pairs trading, where two correlated assets are traded based on their relative performance.

Traders use statistical techniques such as cointegration, correlation, and regression analysis to identify pairs of assets that typically move together. When the prices of these assets diverge, traders bet that they will revert to their historical relationship.

Mean Reversion

Mean reversion strategies are based on the principle that asset prices tend to revert to their historical average or mean over time. These strategies involve identifying overbought or oversold conditions and trading accordingly.

Common indicators used in mean reversion strategies include Bollinger Bands, which measure price volatility and help identify extreme price levels, and the RSI, which indicates whether an asset is overbought or oversold.

Event-Driven Strategies

Event-driven strategies capitalize on market-moving events such as earnings reports, mergers and acquisitions, economic data releases, and geopolitical events. These strategies aim to exploit the temporary price movements caused by such events.

Traders use news sentiment analysis, event studies, and statistical models to predict the impact of events on asset prices and make trades accordingly.

Scalping

Scalping is a high-frequency trading strategy that involves making numerous small trades to capture minor price changes. The goal is to accumulate small, consistent profits throughout the trading day.

Scalpers use advanced algorithms to execute trades within milliseconds, relying on technical indicators such as moving averages, Bollinger Bands, and volume analysis to identify entry and exit points.

Machine Learning-Based Strategies

Machine learning-based strategies leverage advanced data analytics and artificial intelligence to predict market movements and make trading decisions. These strategies can adapt and improve over time as they process more data.

Common machine learning techniques include supervised learning, unsupervised learning, and reinforcement learning. These models analyze vast amounts of historical and real-time data to identify patterns, trends, and anomalies that can inform trading decisions.

APPLICATIONS OF ALGORITHMIC TRADING

Algorithmic trading has become a cornerstone of modern financial markets, revolutionizing how trades are executed and strategies are implemented. It is widely used across various asset classes and by a diverse range of market participants. Here are some key applications of algorithmic trading:

Asset Classes

1. Stocks

Algorithmic trading is extensively used in stock markets to execute large volumes of trades with minimal market impact. Algorithms can quickly respond to market movements, execute trades at optimal prices, and manage risks effectively.

Strategies such as arbitrage, trend following, and market making are commonly applied to stock trading. High-frequency trading (HFT) algorithms are also prevalent, executing numerous trades in milliseconds to capture small price changes.

2. Bonds

The bond market benefits from algorithmic trading through improved liquidity and efficiency. Algorithms help in managing large bond portfolios by automating trade execution and optimizing order placement.

Common strategies include statistical arbitrage and mean reversion, which exploit price discrepancies and yield differentials across different bonds or between bonds and other asset classes.

3. Commodities

In commodity markets, algorithmic trading facilitates the rapid execution of trades in response to price fluctuations driven by supply and demand dynamics, geopolitical events, and economic indicators.

Algorithms are used for trend following, arbitrage between different commodity exchanges, and managing exposure to commodity price risks through futures and options.

4. Currencies (Forex)

The foreign exchange (Forex) market is highly liquid and operates 24/5, making it an ideal environment for algorithmic trading. Algorithms can take advantage of minute price movements and execute trades around the clock.

Popular strategies include trend following, statistical arbitrage, and carry trading, where traders exploit interest rate differentials between currencies.

Understanding algorithmic trading is essential for anyone looking to navigate modern financial markets effectively.

PART: 2: GETTING STARTED WITH ALGORITHMIC TRADING

CHAPTER 4: UNDERSTANDING BASIC TRADING CONCEPTS

Let's now delve into fundamental trading concepts that form the basis of effective trading strategies. For non-programmers venturing into algorithmic trading, grasping these foundational principles is crucial for developing and implementing successful automated trading strategies.

INTRODUCTION TO TRADING CONCEPTS

Trading in financial markets involves various concepts and mechanisms that govern the buying and selling of assets. Understanding these concepts lays the groundwork for constructing robust trading strategies and optimizing trading performance.

A. KEY TRADING CONCEPTS EXPLAINED

Understanding key trading concepts is essential for anyone involved in algorithmic trading. These concepts form the foundation of trading strategies and decision-making processes. Here, we explain some of the most critical trading concepts, focusing on the types of orders used in the market.

Types of Orders

1. Market Orders

Market orders are instructions to buy or sell a security immediately at the current market price. These orders prioritize execution speed over price, meaning they are executed as quickly as possible but without a guarantee of the exact execution price.

Market orders are used when immediate execution is more critical than obtaining a specific price, such as in highly liquid markets where the price is not expected to change significantly in the short term.

2. Limit Orders

Limit orders are instructions to buy or sell a security at a specified price or better. A buy limit order will only be executed at the limit price or lower, while a sell limit order will only be executed at the limit price or higher. This type of order provides control over the execution price but does not guarantee that the order will be filled if the market price does not reach the specified limit.

Limit orders are used when traders want to ensure that they enter or exit a position at a specific price level, allowing for better control over trade execution, especially in volatile markets.

3. Stop Orders

Stop orders, also known as stop-loss orders, are instructions to buy or sell a security once it reaches a specified price, known as the stop price. When the stop price is reached, the stop order becomes a market order and is executed at the best available price. This type of order is used to limit losses or lock in profits.

Stop orders are used to protect against significant losses or to secure profits. For example, a trader holding a long position might set a stop order below the current market price to limit potential losses if the price drops.

4. Stop-Limit Orders

Stop-limit orders combine the features of stop orders and limit orders. Once the stop price is reached, the stop-limit order becomes a limit order rather than a market order. This allows traders to set both a stop price and a limit price, providing control over the execution price even after the stop price is triggered.

Stop-limit orders are used when traders want to avoid the potential slippage of a stop order turning into a market order. For example, a trader can set a stop-limit order to sell if the price drops to a specific level, but only if it can be sold at or above a certain price.

B. OTHER KEY CONCEPTS

1. Bid and Ask Prices

The bid price is the highest price a buyer is willing to pay for a security, while the ask price is the lowest price a seller is willing to accept. The difference between the bid and ask prices is known as the spread.

Understanding bid and ask prices is crucial for executing trades efficiently. The spread can affect the overall cost of trading, particularly in less liquid markets.

2. Liquidity

Liquidity refers to how easily a security can be bought or sold in the market without affecting its price. Highly liquid markets have many buyers and sellers, resulting in tighter spreads and more efficient trading.

Traders prefer liquid markets for quicker execution and reduced transaction costs. Low liquidity can lead to significant price slippage and higher spreads.

3. Slippage

Slippage occurs when there is a difference between the expected price of a trade and the actual price at which it is executed.

This can happen in fast-moving markets or when there is low liquidity.

Traders need to account for slippage, especially when using market orders in volatile markets. Limit orders can help minimize slippage by specifying a maximum acceptable price.

4. Spread

The spread is the difference between the bid price and the ask price of a security. It represents the cost of trading and can vary based on market conditions and the liquidity of the security.

Understanding the spread is essential for calculating trading costs and choosing the appropriate order type. Narrow spreads indicate more competitive pricing and lower transaction costs.

5. Leverage

Leverage involves using borrowed funds to increase the potential return on investment. While leverage can amplify gains, it also increases the risk of significant losses.

Traders use leverage to maximize their exposure to market movements. However, it is crucial to manage leverage carefully to avoid excessive risk and potential margin calls.

6. Margin

Margin refers to the collateral required by a broker to cover the risk of borrowing funds for trading. There are two types of margin: initial margin (the amount needed to open a position) and maintenance margin (the minimum equity required to keep a position open).

Traders must maintain adequate margin levels to avoid margin calls, where the broker demands additional funds to cover potential losses. Understanding margin requirements is vital for effective risk management.

IMPORTANCE OF TRADING CONCEPTS IN ALGORITHMIC

TRADING

In algorithmic trading, mastering key trading concepts is essential for success. These concepts underpin the development, implementation, and optimization of trading strategies. Here's why they are crucial:

Strategy Formulation

Understanding Different Types of Orders and Strategies:

Knowing the various types of orders—such as market orders, limit orders, stop orders, and stop-limit orders—allows traders to design algorithms that can execute trades under different market conditions. Each order type has its specific use case, which can be integrated into the trading strategy to achieve specific objectives.

Application: For example, a trend-following algorithm may use market orders to enter positions quickly during strong market movements, while a mean-reversion strategy might employ limit orders to capitalize on price pullbacks.

Outcome: This understanding enables the creation of robust algorithmic strategies that can adapt to changing market dynamics, enhancing the potential for profitable trades.

Risk Management:

1. Proper Use of Order Types and Strategies

Effective risk management is vital in algorithmic trading to protect capital and ensure long-term profitability. Understanding how different order types can be used to limit risks and manage exposures is fundamental.

Application: Stop orders and stop-limit orders are commonly used to limit potential losses by triggering exits at predetermined price levels. Additionally, strategies like diversification and the use of hedging instruments can mitigate risk.

Outcome: Traders can design algorithms that automatically enforce risk management rules, reducing the emotional impact of trading decisions and protecting against significant market downturns.

2. Maximizing Profitability

By combining various strategies and order types, traders can optimize their algorithms to exploit market opportunities while managing risk. This balance between risk and reward is essential for sustainable trading performance.

Application: For instance, an arbitrage strategy might use market orders for rapid execution to exploit price discrepancies, while a long-term investment strategy could use limit orders to enter positions at favorable prices.

Outcome: Effective risk management and strategic order placement increase the likelihood of capturing profitable trades and maximizing returns.

Execution Efficiency:

1. Knowledge of Trading Concepts for Optimizing Trade Execution

Efficient trade execution is critical in algorithmic trading, where speed and precision can significantly impact profitability. Understanding how different order types function and their impact on execution helps traders select the best orders for their strategies.

Application: In a highly volatile market, using market orders ensures immediate execution but may result in slippage. Conversely, limit orders can control execution prices but may not be filled if the market doesn't reach the specified price. Selecting the appropriate order type based on market conditions and objectives can enhance execution efficiency.

Outcome: Optimized trade execution reduces costs, minimizes slippage, and improves overall trading performance.

2. Adapting to Market Conditions

Markets are dynamic and can change rapidly. Traders who understand key concepts can adjust their algorithms to respond to different market environments effectively.

Application: For example, during periods of low liquidity, using limit orders can prevent significant price impact, while in high liquidity scenarios, market orders can be used for faster execution.

Outcome: Adaptability ensures that trading algorithms remain effective under various market conditions, maintaining consistent performance.

Mastering basic trading concepts is essential for non-programmers entering the world of algorithmic trading.

CHAPTER 5: CHOOSING A TRADING PLATFORM OR SERVICE THAT SUPPORTS ALGORITHMIC TRADING

We will now explore the essential considerations and criteria for selecting a trading platform or service that facilitates algorithmic trading. Choosing the right platform is crucial for non-programmers aiming to automate their trading strategies effectively and efficiently.

INTRODUCTION TO ALGORITHMIC TRADING PLATFORMS

Algorithmic Trading Software & Platforms: wallstreetzen.com

Algorithmic trading platforms provide the infrastructure and tools necessary for non-programmers to develop, deploy, and manage automated trading strategies.

These platforms vary in features, usability, and support, making informed selection vital for successful algorithmic trading endeavors.

Key Considerations for Choosing a Trading Platform

1. User-Friendliness and Interface:

Look for platforms with intuitive interfaces and user-friendly tools that simplify strategy development and deployment. Non-programmers should feel comfortable navigating the platform and accessing necessary features without extensive technical expertise.

2. Supported Assets and Markets:

Ensure the platform supports the assets (e.g., stocks, forex, commodities) and markets (e.g., exchanges, OTC markets) relevant to your trading objectives. This ensures compatibility with your trading strategy and preferred market segments.

3. Automation and Customization:

Evaluate the platform's capabilities for automating trading strategies and customization options. Non-programmers should be able to define and implement their trading rules, parameters, and risk management strategies without complex coding requirements.

4. Backtesting and Optimization Tools:

Robust backtesting functionalities are essential for testing and refining trading strategies against historical market data. Look for platforms that offer comprehensive backtesting tools to assess strategy performance and make data-driven optimizations.

5. Real-Time Data and Execution Speed:

Timely access to accurate market data and fast execution speeds are critical for algorithmic trading success. Choose platforms that provide reliable real-time data feeds and efficient order execution capabilities to capitalize on market opportunities promptly.

6. Security and Reliability:

Prioritize platforms with strong security measures and a reputation for reliability. Ensure the platform employs encryption protocols, offers backup systems, and has a track record of uptime and operational stability.

7. Cost and Fees Structure:

Consider the platform's pricing model, including account fees, transaction costs, and any additional charges for using advanced features or services. Evaluate how costs align with your trading volume and budget constraints.

Research and Comparison

Conduct thorough research and compare multiple platforms based on the above criteria. Look for recommendations from trusted sources such as industry experts and financial advisors. Read reviews and testimonials from other users to gain insights into their experiences and satisfaction levels.

Additionally, take advantage of demo accounts offered by many platforms to test and experience their functionalities firsthand. This hands-on approach will help you make an informed decision and choose the platform that best meets your trading needs and goals.

Choosing the right trading platform is pivotal for non-programmers venturing into algorithmic trading.

By selecting a platform that aligns with their trading goals and preferences, non-programmers can effectively leverage automated strategies to enhance trading efficiency and achieve their financial objectives.

CHAPTER 6: SETTING UP AN ACCOUNT AND ACCESSING MARKET DATA

Let's go through the process of setting up an account and accessing essential market data necessary for algorithmic trading. Understanding how to establish a trading account and obtain reliable market data is foundational for implementing successful automated trading strategies.

INTRODUCTION TO SETTING UP A TRADING ACCOUNT

Setting up a trading account is the initial step towards engaging in algorithmic trading. Whether you're trading stocks, forex, commodities, or other financial instruments, the account setup process typically involves several key steps to ensure readiness for executing trades.

STEPS TO SETTING UP A TRADING ACCOUNT

Choose a Brokerage or Trading Platform:

Select a reputable brokerage firm or trading platform that supports algorithmic trading and aligns with your trading preferences (e.g., asset classes, markets). Consider factors such as fees, commissions, customer support, and available trading tools.

Complete Account Registration:

Follow the brokerage's registration process to open a trading account. Provide required personal information, such as name, address, identification documents, and financial details.

Review and agree to the terms and conditions of the brokerage, including risk disclosures and account management policies.

Fund Your Trading Account:

Deposit funds into your trading account to enable trading activities. Different brokerages offer various funding methods, such as bank transfers, credit/debit cards, or electronic payment systems.

Ensure sufficient funds are available to support your trading strategy and account maintenance requirements.

Accessing Market Data for Algorithmic Trading

Accessing accurate and timely market data is essential for making informed trading decisions and implementing algorithmic strategies effectively. Non-programmers should understand how to obtain and utilize market data to support their trading operations.

SOURCES OF MARKET DATA

Real-Time Data Feeds: Subscribe to real-time market data services provided by your brokerage or third-party data providers. These feeds deliver up-to-the-second pricing information and market updates crucial for algorithmic decision-making.

Historical Data: Utilize historical market data to backtest and optimize trading strategies. Many trading platforms offer historical data repositories that allow users to analyze past market behavior and simulate strategy performance.

DATA ANALYSIS AND INTEGRATION

Data Analysis Tools

Familiarize yourself with the data analysis tools and functionalities offered by your trading platform. These tools are essential for analyzing trends, patterns, and correlations in market data, which can significantly inform and enhance your trading strategies. Key functionalities typically include:

Charting Tools: Visual representations of market data over time, helping you identify trends and potential entry or exit points.

Technical Indicators: Pre-built algorithms like moving averages, RSI, and MACD that provide insights into market conditions and potential future movements.

Customizable Dashboards: Personalized views that allow you to track relevant metrics and indicators in real-time.

Historical Data Analysis: Access to past market data to backtest strategies and understand how they would have performed under different market conditions.

Using these tools effectively can lead to more informed decision-making, better risk management, and ultimately, more successful trading outcomes.

API Integration

For advanced users or developers, exploring the application programming interfaces (APIs) provided by trading platforms can be a game-changer. APIs enable seamless integration of external applications or algorithmic trading bots, allowing for sophisticated data analysis and automated trade execution. Benefits of API integration include:

Automation: Automate repetitive tasks such as data collection, analysis, and trade execution, freeing up time for more strategic decision-making.

Customization: Develop custom algorithms and tools tailored to your specific trading strategies and needs.

Real-time Data Access: APIs provide real-time access to market data, ensuring that your trading decisions are based on the most up-to-date information.

Efficiency: Reduce the potential for human error and increase the speed of trade execution, which is crucial in fast-moving markets.

Scalability: Easily scale your trading operations as your strategies evolve and your requirements grow.

By leveraging API integration, you can enhance the functionality of your trading platform, implement advanced trading strategies, and maintain a competitive edge in the market. Whether you are a seasoned trader or a developer looking to innovate, understanding and utilizing APIs can significantly expand your trading capabilities.

Setting up a trading account and accessing reliable market data are fundamental steps for non-programmers embarking on algorithmic trading.

By establishing a solid foundation in account setup and data access, non-programmers can proceed confidently in implementing automated trading strategies to enhance trading efficiency and achieve their financial goals.

CHAPTER 7: HOW TO INSTALL AND USE EXPERT ADVISORS (EA) ON METATRADER4

In this chapter, we will guide you through the process of finding, installing, and using Expert Advisors (EAs) on MetaTrader 4 (MT4). The assumption is that you have prior experience with manual trading on MT4 and are now looking to leverage automated trading strategies to enhance your trading performance.

WHAT ARE EXPERT ADVISORS (EAs)?

Expert Advisors (EAs) are automated trading scripts written in MetaQuotes Language 4 (MQL4) that can analyze market conditions, generate trading signals, and execute trades based on predefined criteria. EAs allow you to automate your trading strategies, minimizing the need for constant manual monitoring and execution.

WHERE TO FIND EXPERT ADVISORS

There are several sources where you can find Expert Advisors:

1. **MetaTrader Market**: Access the Market tab in your MT4 platform to browse a wide range of EAs available for purchase or free download.

2. **Online Trading Communities**: Websites like MQL5.com,

Forex Factory, and various trading forums offer a variety of EAs shared by other traders.

3. **Brokerage Firms**: Some brokers provide their own EAs or have partnerships with EA developers.
4. **Custom Development**: You can hire a developer to create a custom EA tailored to your specific trading strategy.

HOW TO INSTALL AN EXPERT ADVISOR

Once you have obtained an EA, follow these steps to install it on MetaTrader 4:

Step 1: Download the EA

Download the EA file to your computer. The file should have a .ex4 or .mq4 extension.

Step 2: Copy the EA to MetaTrader 4

1. Open MetaTrader 4.
2. Go to File > Open Data Folder.
3. Navigate to the MQL4 > Experts folder.
4. Copy the EA file into the Experts folder.

Step 3: Restart MetaTrader 4

Close and reopen MetaTrader 4 to ensure the EA is recognized by the platform.

HOW TO ACTIVATE AND USE AN EXPERT ADVISOR

Step 1: Attach the EA to a Chart

1. In the Navigator window, expand the Expert Advisors section.
2. Drag and drop the desired EA onto the chart of the financial instrument you want to trade.

Step 2: Configure EA Settings

1. A settings window will appear, allowing you to customize parameters such as lot size, stop loss, take profit, and other strategy-specific variables.
2. Adjust the settings according to your trading preferences and strategy requirements.

Step 3: Enable Automated Trading

1. Ensure that the AutoTrading button in the toolbar is enabled (it should be green). This allows the EA to execute trades automatically.
2. You can also enable automated trading for individual EAs by checking the "Allow live trading" option in the EA settings window.

Step 4: Monitor and Adjust

1. Monitor the EA's performance on the chart and in the Terminal window, where you can see open trades, account history, and balance.
2. If needed, adjust the EA's settings by right-clicking on the chart, selecting Expert Advisors, and then Properties.

If you need further assistance, you can reach out to your broker for direct help via chat or FAQs. Additionally, experienced traders often share valuable training videos on YouTube that can provide further guidance.

Installing and using Expert Advisors on MetaTrader 4 can significantly enhance your trading efficiency and potential profitability. By following the steps outlined in this chapter, you can effectively set up, configure, and utilize EAs to automate your trading strategies.

PART: 3: EXPLORING SIMPLE TRADING STRATEGIES

CHAPTER 8: INTRODUCTION TO BASIC TRADING STRATEGIES

In this chapter, we introduce fundamental trading strategies that can be effectively implemented without extensive coding knowledge. These strategies are designed to leverage algorithmic trading principles while utilizing user-friendly tools and platforms.

UNDERSTANDING BASIC TRADING STRATEGIES

Trading strategies form the core framework for making trading decisions and executing trades in financial markets. Non-programmers can adopt and implement these strategies using algorithmic trading platforms that offer intuitive interfaces and automation capabilities.

TYPES OF BASIC TRADING STRATEGIES

1. MOVING AVERAGE CROSSOVER:

The moving average crossover strategy is a popular and straightforward method used to identify potential trading opportunities based on the relationship between two moving averages. It involves tracking two different moving averages, typically a shorter-term moving average (e.g., 50-day) and a longer-term moving average (e.g., 200-day). The idea is to generate trading signals when these moving averages cross each other:

CHAPTER 8: INTRODUCTION TO BASIC TRADING STRATEGIES | 39

Moving Average Crossover: dailyfx.com

Buy Signal: When the shorter-term moving average crosses above the longer-term moving average, it indicates a bullish trend. This crossover suggests that the price momentum is shifting upward, and it may be an opportune time to enter a long position.

Sell Signal: Conversely, when the shorter-term moving average crosses below the longer-term moving average, it signals a bearish trend. This crossover suggests that the price momentum is shifting downward, indicating it might be time to exit long positions or enter a short position.

Implementation for Non-Programmers

Implementing the moving average crossover strategy does not require programming skills. Most modern trading platforms offer built-in tools to set up and automate this strategy. Here's how non-programmers can configure and use this strategy:

Select Moving Averages:

Choose Your Moving Averages: Decide on the time periods for your moving averages (e.g., 50-day and 200-day). The choice depends on your trading style and the time frame you are focusing on (short-term, medium-term, or long-term).

Configure Moving Average Indicators:

Access Indicator Tools: On your trading platform, navigate to the indicators section. Select the moving average indicator and set the parameters for the chosen time periods.

Overlay on Chart: Apply the moving averages to your price chart. This will visually display the moving averages and highlight potential crossover points.

Set Up Trading Rules:

Define Crossover Rules: Establish rules for executing trades based on the crossover signals. For example, create a rule that triggers a buy order when the 50-day moving average crosses above the 200-day moving average and a sell order when the 50-day moving average crosses below the 200-day moving average.

Automate the Strategy:

Use Platform Features: Many trading platforms allow you to automate trading strategies using their built-in tools. Set up the automated trading feature to execute buy and sell orders based on your defined crossover rules.

Backtest the Strategy: Before going live, backtest the moving average crossover strategy on historical data. This helps you evaluate its performance and make any necessary adjustments.

Monitor and Adjust:

Regular Monitoring: Keep an eye on the performance of the strategy and the market conditions. While the strategy runs automatically, it's essential to monitor for any significant market changes or anomalies.

Make Adjustments: Based on the performance and market feedback, you may need to adjust the moving average time periods or the rules to better align with current market conditions.

Benefits of the Moving Average Crossover Strategy

Simplicity: This strategy is easy to understand and implement, making it suitable for beginners.

Trend Identification: It helps in identifying trends and provides clear signals for entry and exit points.

Automation: Most trading platforms support this strategy with built-in tools, enabling automated execution without programming.

Backtesting Capability: The strategy can be backtested on historical data to assess its effectiveness before live trading.

2. BREAKOUT STRATEGY:

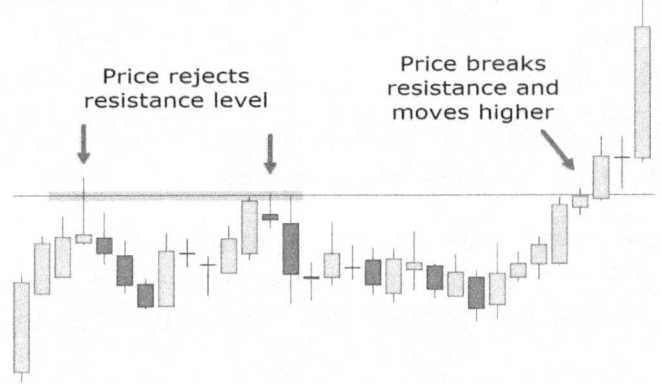

Breakout Trading Strategy: nftcrypto.io

The breakout strategy is a widely used trading approach that focuses on identifying and capitalizing on price levels where an asset's price breaks through significant support or resistance levels. These breakout points often indicate the start of a new trend, offering traders opportunities to enter the market early in the trend's development. Here's a detailed look at how the breakout strategy works:

Support Level: A support level is a price point where an asset tends to find buying interest, preventing it from falling further. When the price breaks below this level, it indicates increased selling pressure and the potential for a further decline.

Resistance Level: A resistance level is a price point where selling interest is strong enough to prevent the price from rising further. When the price breaks above this level, it suggests increased buying interest and the potential for further upward movement.

Buy and Sell Signals

Buy Signal: A buy signal is generated when the price breaks above a defined resistance level. This breakout indicates a potential upward trend, suggesting it may be an opportune time to enter a long position.

Sell Signal: A sell signal occurs when the price breaks below a defined support level. This breakout indicates a potential downward trend, suggesting it might be time to enter a short position or exit long positions.

Implementation for Non-Programmers

Non-programmers can effectively implement the breakout strategy using the charting tools and automated features available on modern trading platforms. Here's a step-by-step guide:

Identify Key Support and Resistance Levels:

Use Charting Tools: Utilize the charting tools on your trading platform to identify historical support and resistance levels. These levels can be drawn manually by looking at price patterns or using built-in indicators like pivot points and trend lines.

Set Alerts: Many platforms allow you to set alerts at specific price levels. Setting alerts can help you monitor when the price approaches these critical levels.

Set Up Conditional Orders:

Define Breakout Conditions: Establish clear conditions for what constitutes a breakout. For example, you might define a breakout as the price closing above resistance or below support by a certain percentage or number of points.

Automate Trade Execution: Use the conditional order features on your trading platform to automate the execution of buy or sell orders when these breakout conditions are met. For instance, set a buy order to trigger when the price breaks above a resistance level and a sell order when it breaks below a support level.

Backtest the Strategy:

Evaluate Historical Performance: Before going live, backtest the breakout strategy on historical data to evaluate its performance. This helps you understand how the strategy would have performed under different market conditions and refine your breakout criteria if necessary.

Monitor and Adjust:

Regular Monitoring: While the strategy can run automatically, it's important to regularly monitor its performance and the market conditions. Adjust your breakout levels and criteria as needed based on market feedback.

Stay Informed: Keep abreast of market news and events that could impact price levels, as breakouts can be influenced by significant news releases or economic events.

Benefits of the Breakout Strategy

Early Trend Identification: The breakout strategy helps traders enter new trends early, potentially maximizing profit opportunities.

Clear Entry and Exit Points: It provides clear and objective entry and exit points based on price action, reducing the reliance on subjective judgment.

Adaptability: The strategy can be applied to various markets, including stocks, forex, commodities, and cryptocurrencies.

Automation-Friendly: Most trading platforms support the automation of breakout strategies, making it accessible to non-programmers.

3. MEAN REVERSION STRATEGY:

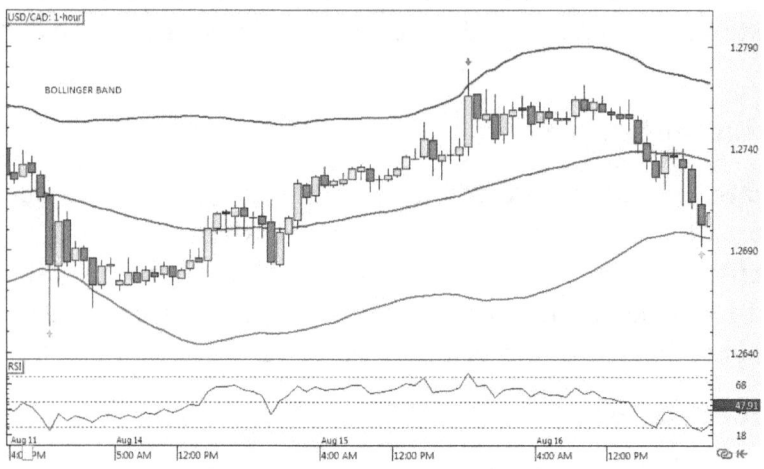

Mean Reversion Strategy: babypips.com

The mean reversion strategy is based on the concept that asset prices tend to revert to their historical average or mean over time after deviating significantly from it. This approach operates under the assumption that prices will return to their normal or average level following extreme movements. Here's how it works in detail:

Oversold Conditions: When an asset's price has fallen significantly below its historical average, it is considered oversold. This condition suggests a potential buying opportunity as the price is expected to revert to its mean.

Overbought Conditions: Conversely, when an asset's price has risen significantly above its historical average, it is considered overbought. This condition suggests a potential selling opportunity as the price is expected to revert to its mean.

Key Technical Indicators

Traders use various technical indicators to identify oversold and overbought conditions, which can signal potential mean reversion opportunities:

Relative Strength Index (RSI): RSI measures the speed and change of price movements and ranges from 0 to 100. An RSI above 70 typically indicates overbought conditions, while an RSI below 30 indicates oversold conditions.

Bollinger Bands: Bollinger Bands consist of a moving average and two standard deviation lines above and below it. Prices touching or exceeding the upper band suggest overbought conditions, while prices touching or falling below the lower band suggest oversold conditions.

Moving Averages: Simple Moving Averages (SMA) or Exponential Moving Averages (EMA) can also indicate mean reversion opportunities when the price deviates significantly from the average.

Implementation for Non-Programmers

Non-programmers can implement mean reversion strategies using the tools and features available on modern trading platforms. Here's a step-by-step guide:

Select Technical Indicators:

Access Indicators: Navigate to the indicators section on your trading platform and select the desired technical indicators (e.g., RSI, Bollinger Bands).

Configure Parameters: Set the parameters for these indicators based on your trading strategy. For instance, set the RSI period to 14 days or adjust the Bollinger Bands to a 20-day moving average with a 2-standard deviation.

Identify Oversold and Overbought Conditions:

Visualize on Chart: Apply the indicators to your price chart to visualize when the asset enters oversold or overbought conditions. This will help you spot potential mean reversion opportunities.

Set Alerts: Set alerts to notify you when the asset reaches these extreme conditions. For example, set an alert when RSI drops below 30 or exceeds 70.

Set Up Automated Trading Rules:

Define Trading Rules: Establish clear rules for entering and exiting trades based on the indicator signals. For instance, create a rule to automatically buy when RSI falls below 30 (indicating oversold) and sell when RSI rises above 70 (indicating overbought).

Automate Orders: Use the conditional order features on your trading platform to automate these trades. Configure the platform to execute buy orders in oversold conditions and sell orders in overbought conditions.

Backtest the Strategy:

Historical Data Analysis: Before implementing the strategy in live markets, backtest it using historical data. Analyze how the strategy would have performed under different market conditions to ensure its effectiveness.

Refine Parameters: Adjust the parameters and rules based on the backtest results to optimize the strategy for current market conditions.

Monitor and Adjust:

Ongoing Monitoring: Regularly monitor the performance of the strategy and make adjustments as needed. Market conditions can change, and it's essential to ensure the strategy remains effective.

Stay Informed: Keep up with market news and trends that

could impact the asset's price movements and mean reversion potential.

Benefits of the Mean Reversion Strategy

Exploits Market Inefficiencies: The strategy leverages the natural tendency of prices to revert to their mean, capitalizing on temporary price extremes.

Clear Entry and Exit Signals: Technical indicators provide clear and objective signals for when to enter and exit trades, reducing reliance on subjective judgment.

Flexibility: Mean reversion can be applied to various asset classes, including stocks, forex, commodities, and cryptocurrencies.

Automation-Friendly: Trading platforms support the automation of mean reversion strategies, making it accessible and efficient for non-programmers.

REAL-WORLD APPLICATIONS

You can apply these strategies across various asset classes, including stocks, forex, commodities, and cryptocurrencies.

These strategies are suitable for both short-term and long-term trading objectives, depending on market conditions and risk tolerance.

Basic trading strategies provide non-programmers with a structured approach to participate in algorithmic trading effectively. This chapter has introduced moving average crossovers, breakout strategies, and mean reversion strategies as accessible options for automated trading. By leveraging user-friendly trading platforms and tools, non-programmers can implement these strategies to enhance trading efficiency, manage risk, and pursue their financial goals.

CHAPTER 9: STRATEGY TEMPLATES OR PRE-CONFIGURED STRATEGIES

In this chapter, we explore strategy templates and pre-configured strategies offered by some trading platforms, providing non-programmers with ready-to-use options to automate their trading activities effectively.

INTRODUCTION TO STRATEGY TEMPLATES AND PRE-CONFIGURED STRATEGIES

Many algorithmic trading platforms provide users, especially non-programmers, with pre-built strategy templates that simplify the process of implementing automated trading strategies. These templates are designed to cater to various trading objectives and market conditions, offering a convenient starting point for traders looking to leverage automation without extensive programming knowledge.

TYPES OF STRATEGY TEMPLATES

1. MOVING AVERAGE CROSSOVER STRATEGIES

Moving average crossover strategies are among the most popular and straightforward templates used in algorithmic trading. These templates automate trading decisions based on the crossover of two moving averages, such as the 50-day and 200-day moving averages. A buy signal is generated when the shorter-term moving average crosses above the longer-term moving average, indicating a bullish trend. Conversely, a sell signal is triggered when the shorter-term moving average crosses below the longer-term moving average, signaling a bearish trend.

You can easily utilize these templates by following these steps:

Select a Moving Average Crossover Template: On your trading platform, choose a moving average crossover template from the available strategy options.

Specify Parameters: Configure the parameters for the moving averages, such as setting the periods to 50-day and 200-day.

Activate the Strategy: Once the parameters are set, activate the strategy. The template will automatically generate buy or sell signals when the specified crossover conditions are met, executing trades based on these signals without requiring manual intervention.

2. BREAKOUT STRATEGIES

Breakout strategy templates are designed to identify price breakouts above resistance levels or below support levels. These strategies capitalize on significant price movements that typically follow a breakout, allowing traders to enter positions early in the new trend. When a breakout occurs, the template triggers automated buy or sell orders to take advantage of the anticipated price movement.

To implement a breakout strategy using a template, non-programmers can:

Choose a Breakout Strategy Template: Select a breakout strategy template from your trading platform's strategy library.

Configure Breakout Levels: Set the specific resistance and support levels that you want the template to monitor for breakouts.

Set Criteria for Order Execution: Define the conditions under which orders will be executed, such as the size of the breakout or the volume of trades accompanying the breakout.

Activate the Template: Once configured, activate the template. It will monitor the market for breakout signals and automatically execute trades when the conditions are met.

3. RSI (RELATIVE STRENGTH INDEX) STRATEGIES

RSI strategy templates use the Relative Strength Index (RSI) indicator to identify overbought or oversold market conditions. The RSI measures the speed and change of price movements on a scale from 0 to 100. Values above 70 typically indicate overbought conditions, suggesting a potential sell opportunity, while values below 30 indicate oversold conditions, suggesting a potential buy opportunity.

You can implement RSI strategies by:

Selecting an RSI Strategy Template: Choose an RSI strategy template from your trading platform's options.

Adjust RSI Thresholds: Set the RSI thresholds based on your trading preferences, such as 30 for oversold conditions and 70 for overbought conditions.

Automate Trades: Configure the template to automatically execute buy orders when the RSI falls below the oversold threshold and sell orders when the RSI rises above the overbought threshold.

Activate the Strategy: Once the thresholds and trade conditions are set, activate the strategy. The template will continuously monitor the RSI and execute trades according to the specified conditions without requiring manual intervention.

By leveraging these strategy templates, non-programmers can effectively implement sophisticated trading strategies with ease. The templates simplify the process of setting up and automating trades based on well-established technical indicators and trading principles, allowing traders to focus on strategy selection and parameter adjustment rather than coding and manual execution.

ADVANTAGES OF STRATEGY TEMPLATES

Ease of Use: Strategy templates eliminate the need for complex coding or algorithm development, making automated trading accessible to non-programmers.

Time Efficiency: Traders can deploy pre-configured strategies quickly, saving time on strategy design and development.

Customization: While templates provide a starting point, many platforms allow for customization of parameters and rules to tailor strategies to specific trading preferences and risk tolerance.

REAL-WORLD APPLICATIONS

Institutional investors and retail traders alike utilize strategy templates to execute trading strategies across diverse asset classes, including stocks, forex, commodities, and indices.

These templates are suitable for both beginners exploring automated trading and experienced traders seeking efficient ways to deploy strategies in dynamic market environments.

Strategy templates and pre-configured strategies offered by trading platforms empower non-programmers to automate their trading activities effectively and efficiently.

By leveraging these templates, non-programmers can

streamline their trading operations, reduce manual intervention, and capitalize on market opportunities with greater confidence.

CHAPTER 10: HOW TO SELECT A STRATEGY THAT ALIGNS WITH YOUR RISK TOLERANCE AND INVESTMENT GOALS

Choosing the right strategy is crucial for optimizing trading performance and aligning automated trading activities with personal preferences. In this chapter, we guide you through the process of selecting an algorithmic trading strategy that suits their risk tolerance, investment objectives, and overall financial goals.

UNDERSTANDING RISK TOLERANCE AND INVESTMENT GOALS

Risk tolerance refers to an individual's willingness and capacity to endure fluctuations in investment returns, particularly in relation to potential losses. Investment goals encompass financial objectives such as wealth accumulation, capital preservation, income generation, or achieving specific benchmarks within a defined timeframe.

FACTORS INFLUENCING STRATEGY SELECTION

1. RISK APPETITE

Your comfort level with risk and market volatility plays

a significant role in strategy selection. Risk appetite varies from individual to individual, depending on factors such as financial situation, investment experience, and psychological disposition.

Considerations:

Conservative Strategies: If you prefer lower risk, conservative strategies such as bond investing, dividend growth investing, or mean reversion might be suitable. These strategies tend to offer lower but more stable returns and minimize exposure to market volatility.

Aggressive Strategies: If you are comfortable with higher risk for the potential of greater returns, aggressive strategies such as trend following, momentum trading, or leverage-based strategies may be appropriate. These strategies can yield higher returns but also come with increased risk of significant losses.

Implementation: Evaluate your personal risk tolerance through self-assessment or risk profiling tools offered by financial advisors or trading platforms. Choose strategies that align with your risk comfort level to ensure you can maintain discipline and emotional control during market fluctuations.

2. TIME HORIZON

Your investment time horizon is the length of time you expect to hold your investments before needing to access the funds. This horizon can range from short-term (months to a few years) to long-term (decades).

Considerations:

Short-Term Traders: If you are focused on short-term gains, strategies such as day trading, swing trading, or breakout trading might be suitable. These strategies aim to capitalize on short-term market movements and require active monitoring and frequent trading.

Long-Term Investors: If your goal is long-term wealth accumulation, strategies such as buy and hold, value investing, or dollar-cost averaging may be more appropriate. These strategies emphasize sustained growth, income generation, and reduced trading frequency.

Implementation: Determine your investment time horizon based on your financial goals and life plans. Align your strategy selection with your time horizon to ensure that your investments can meet your expected returns and liquidity needs without undue stress or risk.

3. FINANCIAL OBJECTIVES

Clearly defined financial objectives help guide strategy selection by aligning your trading activities with your broader financial goals. These objectives can vary widely, including retirement savings, funding education, buying a home, or generating supplemental income.

Considerations:

Retirement Fund: For building a retirement fund, strategies focused on long-term growth and stability, such as index investing or balanced portfolios, are often preferred. These strategies aim to provide steady returns over time with moderate risk.

Education Expenses: If funding education expenses, consider strategies that provide growth with a specific time horizon, such as growth stocks or targeted savings plans. These strategies should align with the timing of your financial needs.

Supplemental Income: To generate supplemental income,

income-focused strategies such as dividend investing or real estate investment trusts (REITs) may be suitable. These strategies provide regular income streams while also offering potential for capital appreciation.

Implementation: Define your financial objectives clearly and evaluate how different strategies can help achieve these goals. Choose strategies that match your expected returns, liquidity needs, and overall portfolio diversification to ensure a cohesive and effective investment plan.

By carefully considering your risk appetite, time horizon, and financial objectives, you can select trading strategies that best suit your personal and financial situation. This thoughtful approach to strategy selection will help you navigate the complexities of the financial markets with greater confidence and effectiveness.

ASSESSING STRATEGY SUITABILITY

Choosing the right trading strategy is a critical step that can significantly impact your investment success. To ensure the chosen strategy is well-suited to your needs, it's essential to assess various factors comprehensively. Here are key considerations for evaluating strategy suitability:

1. STRATEGY CHARACTERISTICS

Understanding the fundamental characteristics of a trading strategy helps in evaluating its potential effectiveness and fit with your investment goals. This involves analyzing several performance metrics and inherent features of the strategy.

Considerations:

Risk-Adjusted Returns: Review how the strategy performs

relative to the risk it takes on. Metrics such as the Sharpe ratio can help measure the risk-adjusted return, indicating how much excess return you receive for the additional volatility endured.

Historical Performance Metrics: Examine the strategy's past performance through various metrics, such as maximum drawdown, which measures the largest peak-to-trough decline during a specific period. This helps in understanding the potential downside risk.

Correlation with Existing Investments: Assess how the strategy correlates with your current investment portfolio. A low or negative correlation can provide diversification benefits, potentially reducing overall portfolio risk.

Implementation: Collect and analyze data on potential strategies from financial reports, backtesting results, and performance analyses. Use this information to compare different strategies and understand how they might impact your overall investment profile.

2. ALIGNMENT WITH RISK TOLERANCE

It's crucial to ensure that the selected trading strategy aligns with your personal risk tolerance. This involves choosing strategies that fit within your comfort zone for potential losses and market volatility.

Considerations:

Risk Comfort Zone: Determine your personal risk tolerance through self-assessment or risk profiling tools. Avoid strategies that exceed your comfort level and could cause undue stress or emotional decision-making during periods of market volatility.

Volatility Tolerance: Evaluate how much market volatility you can comfortably endure. Some strategies may involve frequent and significant fluctuations in value, which might not be suitable for all investors.

Implementation: Match your risk tolerance with the characteristics of potential strategies. Opt for strategies that provide a balanced approach, offering potential returns without exposing you to excessive risk beyond your tolerance level.

3. SCALABILITY AND FLEXIBILITY

Scalability and flexibility are important for accommodating changes in your investment portfolio and adapting to varying market conditions. A scalable and flexible strategy allows for growth and adjustments over time, reflecting evolving goals and market dynamics.

Considerations:

Scalability: Consider whether the strategy can be scaled to handle different portfolio sizes. A scalable strategy can grow with your investment capital, ensuring consistent application regardless of the portfolio's size.

Flexibility: Evaluate the strategy's flexibility to adapt to changes in market conditions and your investment goals. A flexible strategy allows for parameter adjustments and reallocation of assets as needed, maintaining alignment with your risk preferences and financial objectives.

Implementation: Choose strategies that offer scalability and flexibility. Look for options that allow easy modification of parameters and can be applied to varying amounts of capital. This ensures your strategy remains effective as your portfolio grows and market conditions change.

Assessing the suitability of a trading strategy involves a thorough review of its characteristics, alignment with your risk tolerance, and its scalability and flexibility. By carefully evaluating these factors, you can select strategies that not only meet your immediate needs but also adapt to future changes, providing a robust foundation for your investment activities. This thoughtful approach helps ensure that your chosen strategies support your financial goals while managing risk effectively.

IMPLEMENTATION AND MONITORING

Platform Compatibility:

Choose a trading platform that supports the implementation of your selected strategy, providing necessary tools for customization, backtesting, and real-time monitoring.

Periodic Review and Adjustment:

Regularly monitor strategy performance against established benchmarks and review market conditions for potential adjustments. Maintain discipline in adhering to strategy rules and consider periodic rebalancing to optimize portfolio outcomes.

Real-World Application

Non-programmers can utilize strategy selection frameworks and tools provided by trading platforms to evaluate and compare strategies based on risk-return profiles and alignment with personal investment objectives.

Successful implementation of a well-suited strategy can enhance trading efficiency, mitigate risks, and contribute to achieving long-term financial goals.

Selecting an algorithmic trading strategy that aligns with your risk tolerance and investment goals is critical for optimizing trading outcomes and aligning automated trading activities with personal preferences.

By evaluating these factors and leveraging platform tools, non-programmers can confidently deploy strategies that support their financial aspirations while managing risk effectively.

PART: 4: USING TRADING SIGNALS AND INDICATORS

CHAPTER 11: UNDERSTANDING TRADING SIGNALS AND TECHNICAL INDICATORS

In this chapter, we delve into the fundamentals of trading signals and technical indicators, essential tools for analyzing market trends, making informed trading decisions, and enhancing algorithmic trading strategies.

INTRODUCTION TO TRADING SIGNALS

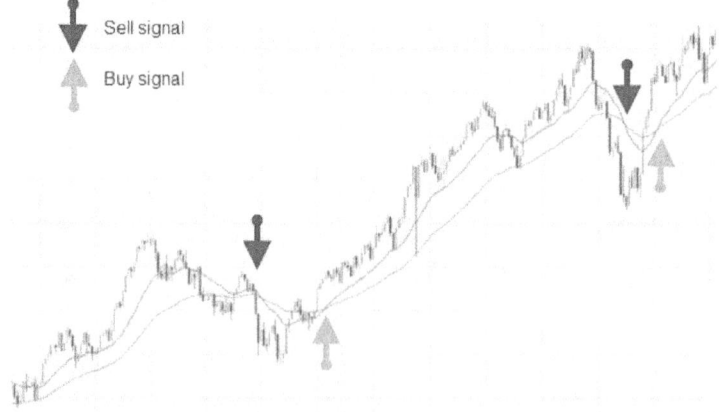

Trading Signals: fxleaders.com

Trading signals are indicators or triggers derived from technical analysis that help traders identify potential buy or sell opportunities in financial markets. These signals are generated based on patterns, trends, or mathematical calculations applied to historical and real-time market data.

Understanding these signals can help traders capitalize on market opportunities while managing risk effectively. Here are the main types of trading signals:

1. BUY SIGNALS

Buy signals are indicators that suggest favorable conditions for purchasing an asset. These signals are typically generated by technical analysis tools, fundamental analysis, or algorithmic criteria that identify potential uptrends or bullish momentum.

Considerations:

Technical Patterns: Buy signals often arise from specific chart patterns, such as head and shoulders, double bottoms, or cup and handle formations. These patterns indicate a potential reversal or continuation of an uptrend.

Oversold Conditions: Indicators like the Relative Strength Index (RSI) or Stochastic Oscillator can signal oversold conditions when their values drop below certain thresholds (e.g., RSI below 30). Oversold conditions suggest that the asset may be undervalued and poised for a price increase.

Bullish Momentum: Moving averages (e.g., 50-day or 200-day) and momentum indicators can generate buy signals when shorter-term averages cross above longer-term averages (golden cross) or when momentum indicators show increasing buying pressure.

Implementation:

Technical Indicators: Non-programmers can configure their trading platforms to monitor technical indicators and generate buy signals based on predefined criteria. For example, setting up alerts for moving average crossovers or RSI values below 30.

Fundamental Analysis: Buy signals can also come from fundamental analysis, such as positive earnings reports, strong economic data, or news that positively impacts the asset's value. Traders can use these insights alongside technical signals to reinforce their buy decisions.

2. SELL SIGNALS

Sell signals indicate conditions that may favor selling an asset. These signals help traders identify potential downtrends, bearish momentum, or overbought conditions, suggesting that it might be time to exit a position to avoid losses or take profits.

Considerations:

Technical Patterns: Sell signals can be derived from chart patterns like head and shoulders, double tops, or rising wedges, which often predict a potential reversal from an uptrend to a downtrend.

Overbought Conditions: Indicators such as RSI or the Stochastic Oscillator can signal overbought conditions when their values rise above certain thresholds (e.g., RSI above 70). Overbought conditions imply that the asset may be overvalued and subject to a price correction.

Bearish Momentum: Moving averages and momentum indicators can generate sell signals when shorter-term averages cross below longer-term averages (death cross) or when momentum indicators show increasing selling pressure.

Implementation:

Technical Indicators: Non-programmers can set up their trading platforms to track technical indicators and trigger sell signals based on predefined conditions. For instance, configuring alerts for moving average crossovers or RSI values above 70.

Fundamental Analysis: Sell signals can also be generated from fundamental analysis, such as negative earnings reports, adverse economic data, or news that negatively affects the asset's value. Combining these insights with technical signals can provide a more comprehensive basis for sell decisions.

Buy and sell signals are critical components of trading strategies, providing traders with actionable insights to optimize their entry and exit points. By understanding and effectively utilizing these signals, traders can enhance their decision-making process, reduce emotional bias, and improve overall trading performance. Whether using technical indicators or fundamental analysis, the ability to interpret and act on these signals is essential for successful trading in the financial markets.

ROLE OF TECHNICAL INDICATORS

Technical indicators are mathematical calculations applied to price, volume, or open interest data to derive trading signals and insights. These indicators help traders interpret market behavior, identify trends, confirm price movements, and predict future price movements based on historical patterns.

COMMON TECHNICAL INDICATORS

1. Moving Averages

Moving averages smooth out price data to create a single flowing line, making it easier to identify the direction of the trend.

Types:

Simple Moving Average (SMA):

Calculates the average price of an asset over a specified number of periods (e.g., 50-day SMA, 200-day SMA).

Purpose: Helps identify the overall direction of the market by smoothing out short-term fluctuations. It's useful for spotting long-term trends.

Implementation: Traders can plot SMAs on their charts and use crossovers (e.g., 50-day SMA crossing above the 200-day SMA) to generate buy or sell signals.

Exponential Moving Average (EMA):

Similar to the SMA, but gives more weight to recent price data, making it more responsive to current price movements.

Purpose: Better suited for identifying short-term trends and trading opportunities due to its sensitivity to recent price changes.

Implementation: Traders use EMAs to capture more timely signals and compare them with SMAs to validate trends and reversals.

2. Relative Strength Index (RSI)

RSI is a momentum oscillator that measures the speed and change of price movements on a scale from 0 to 100.

Purpose:
RSI helps identify overbought or oversold conditions, which can signal potential reversal points in the market.

Implementation:

Overbought Conditions: RSI values above 70 suggest that an asset may be overbought and due for a price correction or pullback.

Oversold Conditions: RSI values below 30 indicate that an asset may be oversold and due for a price rebound.

Trading Strategy: Traders use RSI to time their entries and exits, buying when the RSI indicates oversold conditions and selling when it indicates overbought conditions.

3. Bollinger Bands

Bollinger Bands consist of three lines: a middle band (usually an SMA) and two outer bands that represent standard deviations of price volatility.

Purpose:
Bollinger Bands help identify periods of high and low volatility, as well as potential reversal points.

Implementation:

Price Volatility: When the bands widen, it indicates increased volatility; when they contract, it suggests decreased volatility.

Reversal Points: Prices touching or breaching the outer bands can signal overbought or oversold conditions, potentially leading to reversals.

Trading Strategy: Traders look for price movements that breach the upper or lower bands to identify breakout or reversal opportunities.

4. MACD (Moving Average Convergence Divergence)

MACD is a trend-following momentum indicator that shows the relationship between two moving averages of an asset's price.

Components:

MACD Line: The difference between the 12-day EMA and the 26-day EMA.

Signal Line: A 9-day EMA of the MACD line.

Histogram: The difference between the MACD line and the signal line, visualized as a histogram.

Purpose:
MACD helps identify changes in momentum, trends, and potential reversal points.

Implementation:

MACD Crossovers: A buy signal occurs when the MACD line crosses above the signal line, and a sell signal occurs when it crosses below.

Zero Line Crosses: A cross above the zero line can signal upward momentum, while a cross below can signal downward momentum.

Histogram Analysis: The histogram indicates the strength of the trend; increasing histogram bars suggest strengthening momentum, while decreasing bars indicate weakening momentum.

Understanding and effectively using common technical indicators like Moving Averages, RSI, Bollinger Bands, and MACD can significantly enhance a trader's ability to analyze market conditions and make informed trading decisions. Each indicator has its unique strengths and applications, and combining them can provide a more comprehensive view of market trends and potential trading opportunities.

INTERPRETATION AND APPLICATION

Interpreting and applying technical indicators effectively can significantly enhance trading performance. Here are some key points to consider:

Signal Confirmation

Trading signals generated by technical indicators are often used to confirm buy or sell decisions. This confirmation can reduce the likelihood of false signals and increase the probability of successful trades.

Implementation:

Cross-Validation: Traders can use multiple indicators to validate signals. For example, if both the RSI and MACD indicate a bullish trend, the trader can have more confidence in a buy signal.

Support and Resistance Levels: Confirming signals with support and resistance levels can provide additional validation. For example, a buy signal from an RSI indicator might be more reliable if the asset is also approaching a known support level.

Combination Strategies

Combining multiple technical indicators can enhance the accuracy and reliability of trading signals. This approach leverages the strengths of different indicators to provide a more comprehensive analysis of market conditions.

Implementation:

RSI and MACD: Using RSI to identify overbought or oversold conditions and MACD to confirm momentum can help traders pinpoint optimal entry and exit points. For instance, a trader might wait for the RSI to indicate oversold conditions and then look for a MACD crossover as a buy signal.

Moving Averages and Bollinger Bands: Combining moving averages to identify trends and Bollinger Bands to gauge volatility can help traders execute trades during high-probability breakout or reversal scenarios.

REAL-WORLD APPLICATION

Technical indicators are not just theoretical tools; they have practical applications in real-world trading environments, particularly in algorithmic trading.

Algorithmic Trading Platforms

Algorithmic trading platforms integrate technical indicators and signals, allowing traders to automate their strategies based on predefined conditions and rules.

Implementation:

Automated Strategies: Non-programmers can use these platforms to create and deploy trading strategies without needing to write code. For example, traders can set up a strategy where the platform automatically buys an asset when the RSI indicates oversold conditions and the MACD confirms a bullish crossover.

Backtesting: Algorithmic trading platforms often include backtesting functionalities, allowing traders to test their strategies on historical data to evaluate performance before live trading.

Data-Driven Decisions

Understanding trading signals and technical indicators enables traders to make data-driven decisions, optimizing their trading performance.

Implementation:

Entry and Exit Points: Technical indicators can help traders determine the best times to enter or exit trades, thereby maximizing profits and minimizing losses. For example, a trader might use moving average crossovers to identify entry points and Bollinger Bands to set exit points based on volatility.

Risk Management: Effective use of technical indicators can also enhance risk management. By setting stop-loss orders based on indicator signals, traders can limit potential losses. For instance, a trader might place a stop-loss order if the RSI indicates that an asset has become overbought, suggesting a potential price decline.

Interpreting and applying technical indicators is crucial for successful trading. Signal confirmation and combination strategies enhance the reliability of trading signals, while real-world applications on algorithmic trading platforms allow for the automation of these strategies.

Understanding trading signals and technical indicators equips non-programmers with essential tools to analyze market trends, identify trading opportunities, and enhance algorithmic trading strategies.

CHAPTER 12: HOW TO INTERPRET SIGNALS AND USE THEM IN DECISION-MAKING

Understanding how to interpret signals effectively is crucial for non-programmers seeking to optimize trading outcomes and enhance algorithmic trading strategies. In this chapter, we explore practical techniques for interpreting trading signals derived from technical analysis and integrating them into informed decision-making processes.

INTRODUCTION TO SIGNAL INTERPRETATION

Interpreting trading signals involves analyzing technical indicators, patterns, and market data to gauge market sentiment, identify potential trends, and make timely trading decisions. Non-programmers can leverage these interpretations to automate trading strategies or execute manual trades based on predefined criteria.

STEPS TO INTERPRET SIGNALS

Interpreting trading signals accurately is essential for making informed trading decisions. Here are the key steps involved in this process:

1. REVIEW SIGNAL CHARACTERISTICS

Understanding the specific characteristics and parameters of each technical indicator or pattern is crucial. Different indicators provide various insights into market behavior, and knowing these can help you interpret the signals correctly.

Implementation:

Identify Indicator Purpose: Determine what each indicator measures and the type of signals it generates. For instance, moving average crossovers are used to identify trend changes, while the RSI helps detect overbought or oversold conditions.

Parameter Settings: Understand the default and customizable parameters of each indicator. For example, the period length for moving averages (e.g., 50-day or 200-day) can affect the sensitivity and type of signals generated.

Signal Interpretation: Learn how to read the signals each indicator provides. A moving average crossover might indicate a buy signal when a short-term average crosses above a long-term average, whereas the RSI might suggest a sell signal when it moves above 70, indicating overbought conditions.

2. CONTEXTUAL ANALYSIS

Trading signals should not be interpreted in isolation. Broader market conditions, economic factors, and relevant news events can influence asset prices and the reliability of technical signals.

Implementation:

Market Conditions: Assess the overall market environment. Is it bullish, bearish, or range-bound? Market conditions can affect the performance of different trading strategies and indicators.

Economic Factors: Consider macroeconomic indicators such as interest rates, employment data, and GDP growth, which can impact market trends and sentiment.

News Events: Stay informed about news events that could influence market prices. Earnings reports, geopolitical developments, and major economic announcements can all affect trading signals.

Sector Analysis: Evaluate sector-specific trends and performance. Signals for individual assets can be more reliable if supported by broader sector trends.

3. CONFIRMATION TECHNIQUES

Using multiple indicators or complementary tools to confirm trading signals can reduce the likelihood of false positives and improve the accuracy of your trades.

Implementation:

Combine Indicators: Use different types of indicators to validate signals. For example, if the MACD shows a bullish crossover, you might look for confirmation from the RSI indicating an oversold condition.

Support and Resistance Levels: Validate signals with key support and resistance levels. A buy signal might be more reliable if the asset is near a strong support level.

Volume Analysis: Consider trading volume as a confirming factor. Higher volume on a signal can indicate stronger market interest and increase the reliability of the signal.

Divergence: Look for divergences between indicators and price action. For example, if prices are making new highs but the RSI is not, this might indicate weakening momentum and a potential reversal.

Time Frame Consistency: Confirm signals across multiple time frames. If a signal appears on a daily chart, it can be helpful to check if similar signals are present on weekly or hourly charts.

USING SIGNALS IN DECISION-MAKING

Effectively using trading signals in decision-making is crucial for optimizing trade outcomes. Here are key steps to integrate signals into your trading strategy:

1. DEFINE TRADING RULES

Establishing clear trading rules and criteria based on interpreted signals ensures consistent and disciplined trading decisions.

Implementation:

Entry and Exit Criteria: Define specific conditions for entering and exiting trades. For example, a rule might be to enter a buy position when the 50-day moving average crosses above the 200-day moving average, and exit when the reverse occurs.

Thresholds and Triggers: Set thresholds for indicators that trigger trades. For instance, buy when the RSI falls below 30 (indicating oversold conditions) and sell when it rises above 70 (indicating overbought conditions).

Risk Parameters: Incorporate risk management rules, such as stop-loss and take-profit levels. For example, set a stop-loss order at 2% below the entry price and a take-profit order at 5% above the entry price.

Documentation: Maintain a detailed trading plan that documents all rules and criteria, ensuring clarity and consistency in trade execution.

2. AUTOMATED EXECUTION

Algorithmic trading platforms can automate trade execution

based on predefined signal interpretations and rules, enhancing efficiency and consistency.

Implementation:

Platform Selection: Choose a reliable algorithmic trading platform that supports real-time data feeds and accurate signal processing. Ensure the platform is user-friendly for non-programmers.

Strategy Configuration: Input your trading rules into the platform, specifying the conditions for automatic trade execution. For instance, configure the platform to automatically buy when a moving average crossover occurs.

Backtesting: Use the platform's backtesting feature to evaluate your strategy against historical data. This helps validate the effectiveness of your trading rules before deploying them in live markets.

Monitoring: Continuously monitor the platform's performance to ensure trades are executed as expected. Make adjustments to rules or parameters as needed based on market conditions and strategy performance.

3. MANUAL INTERVENTION

Maintaining the flexibility to override automated decisions or manually execute trades can be beneficial when interpreting unique market conditions or unexpected events not captured by automated strategies.

Implementation:

Manual Overrides: Set up your trading platform to allow manual intervention. This can be useful in scenarios where market conditions rapidly change, and automated rules may not fully capture the new dynamics.

Unique Market Conditions: Be prepared to manually assess and respond to significant market events, such as geopolitical developments or major economic announcements. These events might necessitate a deviation from predefined trading rules.

Hybrid Approach: Consider a hybrid approach where core trading strategies are automated, but manual reviews and adjustments are performed regularly. This combines the efficiency of automation with the adaptability of manual trading.

Education and Training: Continuously educate yourself on market trends and trading techniques. This knowledge will enhance your ability to effectively intervene and make informed decisions when necessary.

Integrating trading signals into decision-making involves defining clear trading rules, leveraging automated execution through algorithmic trading platforms, and maintaining the flexibility for manual intervention..

RISK MANAGEMENT CONSIDERATIONS

Effectively managing risk is crucial in algorithmic trading. Here are key considerations to incorporate into your trading strategy:

Stop-loss and Take-profit Levels

Incorporate stop-loss and take-profit orders to manage risk and secure profits based on signal interpretations.

Implementation:

Stop-loss Orders: Set stop-loss orders to limit potential losses on a trade. For example, if you buy a stock at $100, you might set a stop-loss order at $95 to sell the stock if the price drops to that level, limiting your loss to 5%.

Take-profit Orders: Establish take-profit orders to lock in profits once a trade reaches a target price. For example, if your target profit is 10%, set a take-profit order to sell the stock at $110.

Dynamic Adjustments: Adjust stop-loss and take-profit levels dynamically based on changing market conditions and signal updates. This can involve trailing stop-loss orders that move with the market price to secure gains while minimizing risk.

Position Sizing

Adjusting the size of your positions relative to risk exposure and portfolio diversification goals is crucial for managing overall investment risk effectively.

Implementation:

Risk Per Trade: Determine the percentage of your portfolio you are willing to risk on each trade. For instance, you might decide to risk no more than 2% of your portfolio on a single trade.

Position Size Calculation: Calculate the appropriate position size based on your risk tolerance and the distance to your stop-loss level. For example, if you are risking 2% of a $10,000 portfolio with a $5 stop-loss, you would buy 40 shares ($200 risk / $5 stop-loss).

Diversification: Ensure that your trades are diversified across different assets and sectors to spread risk. Avoid over-concentration in any single asset or market.

Adjustments: Regularly review and adjust position sizes based on changes in portfolio value, market conditions, and individual trade performance.

REAL-WORLD APPLICATION

Non-programmers can apply signal interpretation techniques across various asset classes, including stocks, forex, commodities, and cryptocurrencies, using accessible tools provided by trading platforms.

Enhanced Trading Precision

Optimized Entry and Exit Points: Effective interpretation of signals helps traders identify optimal entry and exit points, improving overall trading precision.

Informed Decision-Making: By combining multiple signals and contextual market analysis, traders can make more informed and confident decisions.

Consistent Performance: Implementing robust risk management strategies ensures consistent trading performance and helps mitigate potential losses, leading to more stable returns over time.

Interpreting trading signals is a fundamental skill for non-programmers aiming to succeed in algorithmic trading.

By mastering signal interpretation and integrating them into decision-making processes, non-programmers can make informed trading decisions, automate strategies effectively, and achieve their financial objectives with confidence.

CHAPTER 13: INCORPORATING SIGNALS INTO YOUR TRADING STRATEGY

Non-programmers can effectively integrate signals into their trading activities using user-friendly tools and platforms. In this chapter, we explore methods for incorporating trading signals derived from technical analysis into your trading strategy, emphasizing approaches that do not require extensive programming knowledge.

INTRODUCTION TO SIGNAL INTEGRATION

Incorporating trading signals involves leveraging technical indicators, patterns, and market data to inform trading decisions and optimize strategy performance. Non-programmers can integrate signals into their trading strategies using accessible methods and platforms designed for algorithmic trading.

STEPS TO INCORPORATE SIGNALS

Incorporating trading signals into your algorithmic trading strategy involves several key steps to ensure effective and efficient execution. Here's an expanded guide to help non-programmers navigate this process:

1. SELECT RELEVANT SIGNALS

Identify and prioritize trading signals based on their relevance to your trading objectives, risk tolerance, and preferred asset classes (e.g., stocks, forex, commodities).

Define Objectives: Start by clarifying your trading goals, whether it's short-term gains, long-term growth, or income generation.

Assess Risk Tolerance: Evaluate your comfort level with risk and potential losses to determine which signals align with your risk appetite.

Choose Asset Classes: Decide which asset classes you want to trade (stocks, forex, commodities, cryptocurrencies) and select signals that are effective for those markets.

Research Signals: Research various technical indicators and patterns to understand their strengths and weaknesses. For example, moving averages are good for trend-following, while RSI is useful for identifying overbought or oversold conditions.

2. PLATFORM TOOLS AND FEATURES

Utilize algorithmic trading platforms offering signal integration capabilities through intuitive interfaces and pre-configured templates. These platforms enable non-programmers to customize parameters, set triggers, and automate trade execution based on interpreted signals.

Steps:

Select a Platform: Choose a trading platform that supports algorithmic trading and offers robust tools for signal integration.

Explore Templates: Many platforms provide pre-configured templates for popular strategies (e.g., moving average crossovers, breakout strategies). Use these templates to get started quickly.

Customize Parameters: Adjust the parameters of the chosen templates to fit your specific needs. For example, set the periods for moving averages or the thresholds for RSI.

Set Triggers: Define the conditions under which trades should be executed. This could include specific price levels, time intervals, or combinations of indicators.

Automate Execution: Enable the platform's automation features to ensure trades are executed automatically when the conditions are met. This reduces the need for constant monitoring and helps capitalize on opportunities promptly.

3. MANUAL REVIEW AND ADJUSTMENT

Regularly review signal performance and strategy outcomes to assess effectiveness and adapt to changing market conditions. Non-programmers can adjust strategy parameters, refine signal interpretation techniques, and optimize trading rules without extensive programming skills.

Monitor Performance: Continuously track the performance of your strategies using the platform's reporting and analytics tools. Look for key metrics such as win rate, average return, and drawdown.

Analyze Results: Assess the effectiveness of your signals and strategies. Identify any patterns or issues that may need adjustment. For instance, a signal that worked well in a trending market may not perform as well in a sideways market.

Adjust Parameters: Based on your analysis, tweak the parameters of your strategies to improve performance. This could involve changing the periods of moving averages, adjusting RSI thresholds, or refining entry and exit criteria.

Stay Informed: Keep up with market trends, economic news, and technological advancements to ensure your strategies remain relevant and effective. Market conditions can change rapidly, and staying informed helps you adapt accordingly.

Seek Feedback: Engage with online communities, forums, or professional advisors to gain insights and feedback on your strategies. Learning from others can provide new perspectives and ideas for improvement.

Incorporating trading signals into your algorithmic trading strategy involves selecting relevant signals, utilizing platform tools and features, and regularly reviewing and adjusting your approach. By following these steps, non-programmers can effectively harness the power of algorithmic trading to achieve their financial goals while managing risk and optimizing performance.

IMPLEMENTING SIGNAL-BASED STRATEGIES

Strategy Customization:

Customize trading strategies by combining multiple signals or integrating additional risk management tools (e.g., stop-loss orders, position sizing) to enhance strategy robustness and adaptability.

Backtesting and Optimization:

Conduct historical backtesting to evaluate signal effectiveness and refine strategy parameters. Algorithmic trading platforms offer backtesting tools that simulate strategy performance using historical market data, allowing non-programmers to validate trading ideas and optimize strategy settings.

Real-Time Monitoring:

Monitor real-time market conditions and signal updates to react promptly to changing trends or emerging opportunities.

Non-programmers can utilize platform features for real-time data analysis, signal alerts, and automated trade execution to maintain trading discipline and capitalize on market dynamics.

RISK MANAGEMENT AND COMPLIANCE

Risk Assessment: Assess potential risks associated with signal-based strategies, including market volatility, unexpected price movements, and execution risks. Implement risk management techniques to mitigate losses and protect capital.

Regulatory Compliance: Adhere to regulatory guidelines and trading rules applicable to algorithmic trading activities, ensuring compliance with market regulations and best practices.

Real-World Application

Non-programmers can effectively incorporate signals into their trading strategies across diverse asset classes using accessible platforms and tools designed for algorithmic trading.

By leveraging signal integration techniques, non-programmers can optimize trading decisions, automate execution based on predefined rules, and achieve consistent performance in algorithmic trading operations.

Incorporating trading signals into your strategy without programming empowers non-programmers to enhance trading efficiency, optimize strategy performance, and achieve financial objectives with confidence.

By mastering signal integration techniques and leveraging platform capabilities, non-programmers can navigate dynamic market conditions, automate trading processes, and capitalize on trading opportunities effectively.

PART: 5: BACKTESTING YOUR STRATEGIES

CHAPTER 14: IMPORTANCE OF BACKTESTING TO EVALUATE STRATEGY PERFORMANCE

Understanding how to effectively conduct backtesting empowers traders, including non-programmers, to optimize their trading strategies and make informed decisions based on historical data analysis. In this chapter, we delve into the significance of backtesting as a crucial tool for evaluating the performance and viability of algorithmic trading strategies.

INTRODUCTION TO BACKTESTING

Backtesting involves simulating trading strategies using historical market data to assess their performance, profitability, and risk characteristics. This process enables traders to validate strategy assumptions, refine parameters, and identify potential strengths and weaknesses before deploying strategies in live trading environments.

BENEFITS OF BACKTESTING

Performance Evaluation: Backtesting provides quantitative insights into strategy performance, including profitability metrics, win/loss ratios, and maximum drawdowns. Traders can analyze historical trades to gauge strategy effectiveness and adjust parameters accordingly.

Risk Assessment: Evaluate risk management techniques within a simulated environment to assess their effectiveness in mitigating potential losses and preserving capital during adverse market conditions.

Strategy Optimization: Identify optimal settings, parameters, and entry/exit criteria through iterative testing and analysis. Backtesting allows traders to fine-tune strategies based on historical data insights, enhancing strategy robustness and adaptability.

Steps to Conduct Effective Backtesting

Backtesting is a crucial process in algorithmic trading, enabling traders to evaluate the performance of their strategies using historical data before deploying them in live markets. Here's an expanded guide to conducting effective backtesting, with examples where possible:

1. DEFINE TRADING STRATEGY

Clearly define the trading strategy, including entry signals, exit signals, position sizing rules, and risk management parameters (e.g., stop-loss levels).

Entry Signals: Specify the conditions under which trades will be initiated. For example, a moving average crossover strategy might enter a buy position when the 50-day moving average crosses above the 200-day moving average.

Exit Signals: Determine the conditions for closing trades. For instance, in the same moving average crossover strategy, you might exit the buy position when the 50-day moving average crosses below the 200-day moving average.

Position Sizing: Establish rules for how much of your portfolio will be allocated to each trade. This could be a fixed percentage of your account balance or a variable amount based on risk factors.

Risk Management: Define stop-loss and take-profit levels. For example, set a stop-loss at 2% below the entry price and a take-profit at 5% above the entry price.

Example: A simple moving average crossover strategy:

- Entry Signal: Buy when the 50-day MA crosses above the 200-day MA.
- Exit Signal: Sell when the 50-day MA crosses below the 200-day MA.
- Position Size: Allocate 2% of the portfolio per trade.
- Stop-Loss: 2% below the entry price.
- Take-Profit: 5% above the entry price.

2. SELECT HISTORICAL DATA

Choose relevant historical market data spanning different market conditions and time periods to ensure comprehensive strategy testing and validation.

Data Sources: Obtain historical price data from reliable sources such as trading platforms, financial data providers, or market databases.

Data Range: Select data that covers various market conditions, including bull markets, bear markets, and periods of high and low volatility. This helps test the robustness of the strategy across different scenarios.

Data Quality: Ensure the data is clean, accurate, and includes all necessary fields (e.g., open, high, low, close prices, and volume).

Example: For testing a stock trading strategy, you might select 10 years of historical price data for major stocks like Apple (AAPL), covering periods like the 2008 financial crisis, the 2013 bull market, and the 2020 COVID-19 crash.

3. EXECUTE BACKTESTING

Utilize algorithmic trading platforms or software with built-in backtesting capabilities to simulate strategy performance. Input strategy parameters and run simulations to generate performance metrics and analyze trade outcomes.

Platform Selection: Choose a platform that offers comprehensive backtesting tools. Popular options include MetaTrader, TradingView, and specialized backtesting software like Amibroker.

Parameter Input: Enter the defined strategy parameters into the platform. This includes the entry and exit signals, position sizing, and risk management rules.

Simulation: Run the backtest by simulating trades based on historical data. The platform will generate performance metrics, including profit and loss, drawdowns, win/loss ratios, and more.

Example: With TradingView, you can easily set up a moving average crossover strategy using Pine Script. Simply follow the platform's step-by-step guide to create the strategy without needing to write code. You can then run a backtest on historical data for a selected stock. TradingView will display performance metrics and show a visual representation of your trades on the price chart.

4. Evaluate Results

Analyze backtest results to assess strategy performance metrics, profitability, drawdowns, and consistency. Identify areas for improvement or adjustment based on performance analysis and statistical measures.

Performance Metrics: Review key metrics such as total return, annualized return, maximum drawdown, Sharpe ratio, and win rate.

Profitability: Assess the overall profitability of the strategy. Look at net profit, profit factor (gross profit divided by gross loss), and the number of winning versus losing trades.

Drawdowns: Examine drawdown periods to understand the risk and potential for significant losses. A high maximum drawdown may indicate the need for improved risk management.

Consistency: Evaluate the consistency of returns over different time periods. A strategy with consistent performance is generally more reliable.

Optimization: Based on the results, fine-tune the strategy parameters. This might involve adjusting moving average periods, stop-loss levels, or position sizes to enhance performance.

Example: After running the moving average crossover strategy on Apple (AAPL) data, you might find:

- Total Return: 150%
- Annualized Return: 10%
- Maximum Drawdown: 20%
- Sharpe Ratio: 1.2
- Win Rate: 55%

If the maximum drawdown is too high, consider tighter stop-loss levels or smaller position sizes to reduce risk.

Effective backtesting involves defining a clear trading strategy, selecting comprehensive historical data, executing simulations on a reliable platform, and thoroughly evaluating the results.

Backtesting is a fundamental process for evaluating the performance and viability of algorithmic trading strategies.

By mastering backtesting techniques and leveraging historical data insights, non-programmers can refine their trading strategies, mitigate potential risks, and achieve consistent performance in algorithmic trading activities

CHAPTER 15: TOOLS AND PLATFORMS THAT OFFER BACKTESTING FUNCTIONALITIES

In this chapter, we explore various tools and platforms equipped with backtesting functionalities, essential for traders, including non-programmers, to evaluate and optimize algorithmic trading strategies using historical market data.

IMPORTANCE OF BACKTESTING TOOLS

Backtesting tools enable traders to simulate trading strategies using historical data, assess performance metrics, and refine strategies based on quantitative analysis. These tools facilitate informed decision-making, strategy optimization, and risk management in algorithmic trading operations.

CRITERIA FOR SELECTING BACKTESTING TOOLS

Selecting the right backtesting tools is crucial for developing and validating your trading strategies. Here are key criteria to consider:

1. HISTORICAL DATA AVAILABILITY

Choose platforms offering comprehensive historical data across asset classes (e.g., stocks, forex, commodities) and varying timeframes to ensure robust strategy testing.

Data Variety: Ensure the tool provides extensive historical data for multiple asset classes to test strategies across different markets.

Data Quality: Look for platforms offering accurate and reliable data, including price, volume, and other relevant metrics.

Timeframes: Access to long-term data is essential for understanding how strategies perform over different market cycles, including bull and bear markets.

2. EASE OF USE

Prioritize user-friendly interfaces and intuitive features that simplify strategy parameter input, simulation setup, and result interpretation, catering to non-programmers' needs.

User Interface: The platform should have a clean, intuitive interface that makes it easy to input strategy parameters and set up simulations.

Guides and Tutorials: Availability of comprehensive guides, tutorials, and customer support to assist users in navigating the tool and understanding its functionalities.

Visualization: Tools that offer clear visual representations of backtest results, such as charts and graphs, to help users easily interpret performance metrics.

3. CUSTOMIZATION AND FLEXIBILITY

Select tools allowing customization of strategy parameters, testing scenarios, and performance metrics to align with specific trading objectives and risk preferences.

Parameter Adjustments: The ability to customize parameters such as entry and exit criteria, position sizing, and risk management rules.

Scenario Testing: Features that allow testing under various market conditions and scenarios to evaluate strategy robustness.

Performance Metrics: Access to detailed performance metrics, including profit and loss, drawdowns, Sharpe ratio, and other key indicators.

When selecting backtesting tools, focus on historical data availability, ease of use, and customization capabilities. These criteria ensure that the tool you choose will be comprehensive, accessible, and adaptable to your specific trading needs and objectives.

POPULAR BACKTESTING TOOLS AND PLATFORMS

MetaTrader 4 (MT4) and MetaTrader 5 (MT5):

Features: MT4 and MT5 platforms offer built-in backtesting capabilities, supporting automated trading strategies using MQL (MetaQuotes Language). Traders can access historical data, optimize Expert Advisors (EAs), and analyze strategy performance metrics.

Asset Classes: Widely used for forex trading, with additional support for stocks, indices, and commodities through third-party plugins.

TradingView:

Features: TradingView provides a web-based platform with integrated backtesting tools and a vast library of technical indicators. Traders can backtest strategies across multiple asset classes, visualize results with interactive charts, and share ideas within a community-driven environment.

Accessibility: Suitable for traders seeking intuitive charting tools and social trading features without requiring extensive programming skills.

QuantConnect:

Features: QuantConnect is a cloud-based algorithmic trading platform offering backtesting, live trading, and strategy development tools. It supports multiple programming languages (C#, Python) and provides access to historical market data, strategy optimization, and community-driven algorithm sharing.

Integration: Ideal for developers and non-programmers alike, facilitating strategy deployment across equities, forex, cryptocurrencies, and derivatives markets.

Backtrader:

Features: Backtrader is a Python-based open-source framework for backtesting and live trading strategies. It offers flexibility in strategy development, integration with external data sources, and visualization of performance metrics through customizable plots and reports.

Community Support: Suitable for Python enthusiasts and algorithmic traders seeking extensive customization and integration capabilities.

BENEFITS OF USING BACKTESTING TOOLS

Backtesting tools provide a multitude of benefits that are essential for both novice and experienced traders. Here's an in-depth look at the key advantages:

1. PERFORMANCE EVALUATION

Assess strategy profitability, risk-adjusted returns, and consistency across different market conditions.

Profitability Analysis: By simulating a trading strategy using historical data, traders can evaluate how profitable the strategy would have been in the past, offering insights into its potential future performance.

Risk-Adjusted Returns: Tools often calculate metrics such as the Sharpe ratio, which helps in understanding the return of an investment compared to its risk. This is crucial for determining whether a strategy's returns are worth the risks taken.

Consistency: Backtesting allows traders to see how consistently a strategy performs over different market conditions, including bull, bear, and sideways markets. This helps in assessing whether a strategy is robust and reliable.

Example: A trader using a backtesting tool might discover that a momentum-based strategy performs well in trending markets but poorly during periods of high volatility, leading to adjustments or alternative strategies for different market phases.

2. STRATEGY OPTIMIZATION

Fine-tune parameters, adjust risk management techniques, and identify optimal entry/exit points based on backtest results.

Parameter Adjustment: Backtesting tools allow traders to experiment with different parameters (e.g., moving average periods, stop-loss levels) to find the optimal settings that maximize performance.

Risk Management Techniques: Traders can test various risk management approaches, such as different stop-loss levels or position sizing strategies, to minimize potential losses and maximize gains.

Entry/Exit Points: By analyzing backtest results, traders can identify the most effective entry and exit points for their trades, enhancing the precision and timing of their strategy execution.

Example: After backtesting a moving average crossover strategy, a trader might determine that a 20-day/50-day crossover yields better results than a 10-day/30-day crossover, leading to more informed adjustments.

3. Educational Resources

Many platforms offer educational resources, tutorials, and community forums to support traders in learning backtesting techniques and refining algorithmic trading strategies.

Tutorials and Guides: Comprehensive tutorials and guides help traders understand how to effectively use backtesting tools and interpret the results, making the process accessible even for non-programmers.

Community Forums: Many platforms have active user communities where traders can share insights, ask questions, and learn from each other's experiences, fostering a collaborative learning environment.

Webinars and Courses: Some platforms provide webinars, courses, and workshops led by experienced traders and professionals, offering deeper insights into advanced backtesting techniques and algorithmic trading strategies.

Backtesting tools and platforms play a pivotal role in evaluating and refining algorithmic trading strategies using historical market data.

By leveraging these tools effectively, non-programmers can enhance trading precision, validate trading ideas, and achieve consistent performance in dynamic market environments.

CHAPTER 16: INTERPRETING BACKTEST RESULTS AND REFINING STRATEGIES BASED ON FINDINGS

In this chapter, we explore the critical process of interpreting backtest results to evaluate strategy performance and refine algorithmic trading strategies effectively. Understanding how to analyze and interpret findings from backtesting empowers traders, including non-programmers, to optimize their trading strategies and enhance decision-making capabilities.

IMPORTANCE OF INTERPRETING BACKTEST RESULTS

Interpreting backtest results is essential for assessing strategy effectiveness, identifying potential improvements, and making informed adjustments to optimize trading performance. This process involves analyzing performance metrics, evaluating risk management techniques, and refining strategy parameters based on empirical data insights.

STEPS TO INTERPRET BACKTEST RESULTS

Interpreting backtest results is crucial for understanding the effectiveness and potential of a trading strategy. Here are the essential steps to thoroughly analyze and interpret these results:

1. PERFORMANCE METRICS ANALYSIS

Evaluate key performance metrics such as total return, average return per trade, Sharpe ratio, and maximum drawdown to gauge strategy profitability and risk-adjusted returns.

Total Return: Measure the overall profit or loss generated by the strategy over the backtested period.

Average Return per Trade: Assess the average profit or loss per trade, providing insights into the efficiency of the strategy.

Sharpe Ratio: Evaluate the risk-adjusted return by comparing the strategy's excess return over the risk-free rate to its standard deviation. A higher Sharpe ratio indicates better risk-adjusted performance.

Maximum Drawdown: Identify the largest peak-to-trough decline in the strategy's value, highlighting the potential risk of significant losses.

Example: A strategy with a high total return but a low Sharpe ratio might indicate substantial profits accompanied by high risk, requiring further refinement to improve risk-adjusted returns.

2. RISK ASSESSMENT

Assess risk metrics, including volatility measures, maximum drawdowns, and recovery periods, to understand potential downside risk and resilience of the strategy during adverse market conditions.

Volatility Measures: Analyze the standard deviation of returns to understand the strategy's variability and potential risk.

Maximum Drawdowns: Evaluate the deepest and longest drawdowns to understand the worst-case scenarios and the strategy's vulnerability during market downturns.

Recovery Periods: Assess how quickly the strategy recovers from drawdowns, providing insights into its resilience and ability to rebound after losses.

Example: A strategy with frequent and deep drawdowns but quick recovery periods might be suitable for risk-tolerant traders, while those preferring stability might seek strategies with smaller drawdowns and steady growth.

3. TRADE ANALYSIS

Review trade-level data, including entry/exit points, trade duration, and trade outcomes (profitable vs. losing trades), to identify patterns, trends, and areas for improvement in strategy execution.

Entry/Exit Points: Analyze the timing of trades to determine if the strategy captures optimal market conditions.

Trade Duration: Evaluate how long trades are held to understand the strategy's time horizon and turnover rate.

Trade Outcomes: Assess the ratio of profitable to losing trades, as well as the magnitude of gains and losses, to identify potential adjustments for improving success rates.

Example: If the majority of losing trades are due to poor timing of exits, the strategy might benefit from revised exit rules or trailing stop-losses to capture more profits.

4. COMPARATIVE ANALYSIS

Compare backtest results against benchmark indices or alternative strategies to benchmark performance, validate strategy assumptions, and assess competitive advantage in achieving trading objectives.

Benchmark Indices: Compare the strategy's performance to relevant market benchmarks (e.g., S&P 500, NASDAQ) to assess relative performance.

Alternative Strategies: Analyze how the strategy performs compared to other strategies with similar objectives, providing a competitive context.

Validation: Ensure that the strategy's assumptions hold true across different market conditions and that the strategy can outperform benchmarks consistently.

Example: A strategy that consistently outperforms the S&P 500 during both bull and bear markets indicates strong competitive advantage and robustness, validating its potential for real-world application.

Interpreting backtest results involves a comprehensive evaluation of performance metrics, risk assessment, trade analysis, and comparative analysis.

REFINING STRATEGIES BASED ON FINDINGS

Refining your trading strategies based on backtest findings is an essential step to improve their effectiveness and robustness. Here are key steps to consider for optimizing your strategies:

1. PARAMETER OPTIMIZATION

Adjust strategy parameters, including entry/exit criteria, position sizing rules, and risk management techniques, based on insights gained from backtest analysis. Fine-tuning parameters can enhance strategy robustness and adaptability across varying market conditions.

Entry/Exit Criteria: Modify the conditions under which trades are initiated and closed. For example, adjusting the moving average periods in a crossover strategy or tweaking RSI thresholds.

Position Sizing Rules: Optimize how much capital is allocated to each trade based on risk tolerance and potential returns. This might involve adjusting the percentage of the portfolio invested per trade or using volatility-based position sizing.

Risk Management Techniques: Refine stop-loss levels, take-profit points, and trailing stops to better protect against losses while capturing profits.

Example: If backtesting reveals frequent stop-loss triggers during minor market corrections, adjusting stop-loss levels to accommodate short-term volatility may prevent premature exits and improve overall returns.

2. SCENARIO TESTING

Conduct scenario-based testing by simulating strategy performance under different market scenarios, economic conditions, or asset class movements. This iterative process helps anticipate strategy performance variability and optimize decision-making strategies.

Market Scenarios: Test the strategy under various market conditions, such as bull markets, bear markets, and sideways trends. This helps in understanding how the strategy performs under different market environments.

Economic Conditions: Simulate the impact of economic events like interest rate changes, inflation spikes, or geopolitical events to assess how sensitive the strategy is to external factors.

Asset Class Movements: Evaluate the strategy's performance across different asset classes (e.g., equities, forex, commodities) to ensure it's versatile and adaptable.

Example: If a strategy performs well in trending markets but poorly in volatile conditions, incorporating volatility filters or switching to a mean-reversion approach during high volatility periods can enhance performance.

3. ITERATIVE IMPROVEMENT

Implement iterative improvement cycles to refine strategy components, incorporate new data insights, and validate adjustments through subsequent backtesting iterations. Continual refinement enhances strategy effectiveness and responsiveness to market dynamics.

Refinement Cycles: Regularly review and adjust the strategy based on new data and backtest results. This continuous feedback loop ensures the strategy evolves with changing market conditions.

Incorporate New Data: Use the latest market data and insights from recent backtests to refine strategy rules. This might involve integrating new technical indicators or adjusting existing ones.

Validation: After making adjustments, conduct new rounds of backtesting to validate the changes. Ensure that the refined strategy performs better or more consistently than the previous version.

Example: After backtesting a strategy with updated parameters, if the results show reduced drawdowns and improved Sharpe ratios, the refined strategy is likely more robust. Further testing can help confirm its reliability before deploying in live markets.

Refining trading strategies based on backtest findings involves a systematic approach to parameter optimization, scenario testing, and iterative improvement. By fine-tuning entry/exit criteria, position sizing, and risk management techniques, you can enhance strategy performance across various market conditions.

Scenario testing further ensures robustness by evaluating how strategies perform under different economic and market scenarios. Continuous iterative improvement, driven by new data and backtest validations, ensures that strategies remain effective and responsive to evolving market dynamics. This comprehensive refinement process is crucial for maximizing profitability and minimizing risks in algorithmic trading.

Interpreting backtest results and refining strategies based on empirical findings are essential steps for optimizing algorithmic trading strategies and achieving trading objectives effectively.

By mastering backtest interpretation techniques and leveraging data-driven insights, non-programmers can refine their trading strategies, mitigate potential risks, and capitalize on trading opportunities with confidence.

PART: 6: MANAGING RISK IN ALGORITHMIC TRADING

CHAPTER 17: RISK MANAGEMENT PRINCIPLES

In this chapter, we explore essential risk management principles tailored for non-programmers engaging in algorithmic trading. Effective risk management is critical for preserving capital, mitigating potential losses, and achieving sustainable long-term success in trading activities.

IMPORTANCE OF RISK MANAGEMENT

Risk management is the process of identifying, assessing, and prioritizing risks followed by coordinated efforts to minimize, monitor, and control the probability or impact of unfortunate events. In algorithmic trading, sound risk management practices ensure prudent decision-making, protect against unexpected market movements, and maintain trading discipline.

KEY RISK MANAGEMENT PRINCIPLES

Effective risk management is crucial for success in algorithmic trading. Here are key principles to help you manage risk and protect your capital:

1. DEFINE RISK TOLERANCE

Establish a clear understanding of your risk tolerance level, considering factors such as financial goals, investment horizon, and comfort with market volatility. Define acceptable levels of risk exposure aligned with your trading objectives.

Financial Goals: Determine whether your primary aim is capital preservation, income generation, or aggressive growth.

Investment Horizon: Consider the length of time you plan to hold investments. Short-term traders may tolerate more volatility, while long-term investors might prioritize stability.

Market Volatility Comfort: Assess how much price fluctuation you can endure without panic-selling. This psychological aspect is crucial for maintaining discipline.

Example: An investor with a long-term horizon and moderate risk tolerance might allocate a smaller portion of their portfolio to high-volatility assets like cryptocurrencies and a larger portion to stable, blue-chip stocks.

2. DIVERSIFICATION STRATEGY

Diversify your portfolio across different asset classes, industries, and geographic regions to spread risk and reduce exposure to specific market fluctuations. Avoid overconcentration in a single asset or sector to mitigate potential losses.

Asset Classes: Include a mix of stocks, bonds, commodities, and real estate.

Industries: Spread investments across various sectors such as technology, healthcare, finance, and consumer goods.

Geographic Regions: Invest in markets across different countries and regions to reduce country-specific risks.

Example: A diversified portfolio might include U.S. equities, emerging market bonds, European real estate, and gold. This reduces the impact of a downturn in any single market.

3. Position Sizing Rules

Implement position sizing rules to allocate capital effectively and manage risk per trade. Determine the maximum percentage of capital to risk per trade (e.g., using fixed percentage or volatility-based methods) to safeguard against excessive losses.

Fixed Percentage Method: Risk a set percentage of your capital on each trade, such as 1-2%.

Volatility-Based Method: Adjust position sizes based on asset volatility, risking more on stable assets and less on volatile ones.

Example: If you have a $100,000 portfolio and decide to risk 2% per trade, you would limit your potential loss to $2,000 for each trade.

4. Use Stop-loss Orders

Utilize stop-loss orders to automatically exit positions if market prices move against your expectations. Set stop-loss levels based on technical analysis, volatility metrics, or predefined risk thresholds to limit potential losses and protect capital.

Technical Analysis: Place stop-loss orders at key support or resistance levels identified through chart analysis.

Volatility Metrics: Use Average True Range (ATR) to set stop-loss levels that account for normal price fluctuations.

Example: If you buy a stock at $100 and set a stop-loss at $95 based on a technical support level, the trade will automatically close if the price drops to $95, limiting your loss to $5 per share.

5. Monitor and Adjust Risk Parameters

Regularly monitor portfolio performance, market conditions, and strategy outcomes to assess risk exposure. Adjust risk parameters, such as position sizes or stop-loss levels, based on changing market dynamics or new data insights derived from performance analysis.

Performance Monitoring: Track the performance of your trades and overall portfolio to identify trends and areas for improvement.

Market Condition Adjustment: Adapt your risk management strategies to reflect current market conditions, such as increasing cash holdings during periods of high volatility.

Example: If you notice that your current stop-loss levels are being triggered frequently due to increased market volatility, you might adjust them to account for this heightened volatility, thereby reducing the number of premature exits.

Implementing these key risk management principles will help you safeguard your capital, manage risk exposure, and achieve your trading objectives.

Practical Risk Management Techniques

Incorporating effective risk management techniques into your trading approach is essential for long-term success and sustainability. Here are some practical techniques to help you manage risk effectively:

1. RISK-REWARD RATIO

Evaluate risk-reward ratios for each trade to assess potential profitability relative to potential losses. Aim for favorable risk-reward ratios (e.g., 2:1 or higher) to justify trade entries and ensure potential gains outweigh potential risks.

Risk-Reward Calculation: Determine the potential risk by identifying the distance from your entry point to your stop-loss level, and the potential reward by measuring the distance from your entry point to your target price.

Favorable Ratios: Aim for a risk-reward ratio of at least 2:1, meaning you stand to gain twice as much as you risk losing.

Example: If you enter a trade at $100, set a stop-loss at $95 (risking $5), and have a target price of $110 (potential reward of $10), the risk-reward ratio is 2:1.

2. STRESS TESTING AND SCENARIO ANALYSIS

Conduct stress testing and scenario analysis to simulate portfolio performance under adverse market conditions or extreme scenarios. Identify vulnerabilities, assess strategy resilience, and implement contingency plans to mitigate downside risks.

Stress Testing: Simulate extreme market events, such as sudden market crashes or unexpected economic changes, to see how your portfolio would perform.

Scenario Analysis: Create various market scenarios (e.g., rising interest rates, geopolitical instability) to test how different conditions impact your trading strategies.

Example: Simulate the 2008 financial crisis conditions to see how your current portfolio would have fared and adjust your risk management strategies accordingly.

3. REGULAR PERFORMANCE REVIEW

Perform regular performance reviews and post-trade analysis to evaluate strategy effectiveness, identify risk factors, and validate risk management practices. Learn from past mistakes and refine risk management strategies accordingly.

Performance Metrics: Track key performance metrics such as win rate, average profit/loss per trade, and drawdowns.

Post-Trade Analysis: Review each trade to understand what worked and what didn't, focusing on how well your risk management strategies protected your capital.

Example: After each quarter, review your trading performance, noting instances where your stop-losses were hit or where trades exceeded expected returns. Use this information to refine your stop-loss placements and improve your risk-reward assessments.

Implementing these practical risk management techniques will help you navigate the complexities of trading with greater confidence and control.

Effective risk management is essential for non-programmers engaging in algorithmic trading to safeguard capital, optimize trading outcomes, and achieve long-term financial goals.

By implementing these principles and adapting to changing market dynamics, non-programmers can mitigate risks effectively, capitalize on trading opportunities, and foster resilience in their algorithmic trading endeavors.

CHAPTER 18: SETTING UP STOP-LOSS ORDERS AND OTHER RISK CONTROL MEASURES

In this chapter, we delve into practical strategies for setting up stop-loss orders and implementing other risk control measures essential for non-programmers in algorithmic trading. These risk management techniques help protect capital, manage downside risk, and enhance trading discipline in dynamic market environments.

IMPORTANCE OF STOP-LOSS ORDERS

Stop-loss orders are critical risk management tools that automatically trigger trade execution to limit losses when market prices move against your trading position. Implementing stop-loss orders ensures disciplined risk management and protects against adverse market movements that could erode capital.

STEPS TO SET UP STOP-LOSS ORDERS

Setting up stop-loss orders is a crucial risk management technique that helps traders limit potential losses and protect their capital. Here are the steps to effectively set up stop-loss orders:

1. DEFINE RISK TOLERANCE

Assess your risk tolerance level and establish acceptable levels of potential loss per trade. Determine the maximum percentage of capital you are willing to risk on each trade, considering your overall investment strategy and financial goals.

Personal Risk Tolerance: Understand your comfort level with potential losses and market volatility.

Capital Allocation: Decide on the maximum percentage of your trading capital you are willing to risk on a single trade. Common guidelines suggest risking no more than 1-3% of your total capital per trade.

Example: If you have $10,000 in trading capital and decide to risk 2% per trade, your maximum loss per trade would be $200.

2. TECHNICAL ANALYSIS FOR STOP-LOSS PLACEMENT

Use technical analysis tools, such as support/resistance levels, moving averages, or volatility indicators, to identify optimal stop-loss placement. Adjust stop-loss levels based on market volatility, trade duration, and risk-reward considerations.

Support and Resistance Levels: Place stop-loss orders just below support levels for long positions or above resistance levels for short positions.

Moving Averages: Use moving averages to identify trends and set stop-loss orders just below a moving average for long positions or above a moving average for short positions.

Volatility Indicators: Consider volatility indicators like the Average True Range (ATR) to set stop-loss levels that account for typical price fluctuations.

Example: If you are trading a stock with a support level at

$50, you might place your stop-loss at $49 to protect against a significant drop below this level.

3. PLACEMENT STRATEGIES

Choose appropriate stop-loss placement strategies to suit your trading style and market conditions.

Percentage-based Stop-Loss: Set stop-loss levels as a percentage of the entry price (e.g., 1% to 3% of capital per trade) to maintain consistency in risk exposure across trades.

Volatility-based Stop-Loss: Adjust stop-loss levels based on asset volatility, incorporating measures like the Average True Range (ATR) or standard deviation to reflect market conditions and price fluctuations.

Example: If a stock is trading at $100 and you use a 2% stop-loss, your stop-loss order would be placed at $98. Alternatively, if the ATR is $3, you might set your stop-loss $3 below the entry price, at $97.

4. CONTINUOUS MONITORING AND ADJUSTMENT

Regularly monitor market conditions, price movements, and strategy performance to evaluate the effectiveness of stop-loss orders. Adjust stop-loss levels dynamically based on changing market dynamics or new data insights derived from performance analysis.

Market Monitoring: Keep an eye on market news, price movements, and economic indicators that might affect your trades.

Adjusting Stop-Losses: As the trade progresses, consider moving your stop-loss order to a breakeven point or beyond to lock in profits (also known as a trailing stop-loss).

Example: If a stock you bought at $100 has moved up to $110, you might adjust your stop-loss from $95 to $105 to lock in a $5 profit while still allowing room for the trade to grow.

Setting up stop-loss orders involves a combination of understanding your risk tolerance, applying technical analysis, choosing appropriate placement strategies, and continuously monitoring and adjusting your positions.

OTHER RISK CONTROL MEASURES

Position Sizing:

Implement position sizing rules to allocate capital proportionally to each trade based on risk assessment and strategy parameters. Adjust position sizes to align with risk tolerance and optimize risk-adjusted returns.

Portfolio Diversification:

Diversify your portfolio across different asset classes, industries, or geographic regions to spread risk and reduce exposure to specific market fluctuations. Avoid overconcentration in a single asset to mitigate potential losses.

Contingency Plans and Exit Strategies:

Develop contingency plans and exit strategies for unexpected market events or adverse scenarios. Define criteria for exiting trades based on predefined risk thresholds, performance targets, or adverse market conditions to protect capital.

Integrating Risk Control Measures

You can integrate stop-loss orders and other risk control measures into algorithmic trading strategies using user-friendly platforms and tools offering automated execution, risk assessment, and position sizing calculators.

By prioritizing risk control measures, traders can enhance trading discipline, manage downside risk effectively, and navigate volatile market conditions with confidence, fostering sustainable trading success in algorithmic trading operations.

Setting up stop-loss orders and implementing effective risk control measures are essential practices for non-programmers in algorithmic trading to protect capital, manage risk exposure, and optimize trading outcomes.

By incorporating these techniques into trading strategies and adapting to market dynamics, non-programmers can mitigate risks, capitalize on trading opportunities, and achieve long-term financial objectives in algorithmic trading.

CHAPTER 19: STRATEGIES FOR DIVERSIFICATION AND PORTFOLIO MANAGEMENT

Diversification helps spread risk across different asset classes, industries, and geographic regions, enhancing portfolio resilience and optimizing risk-adjusted returns. In this chapter, we explore essential strategies for diversifying your investment portfolio and managing it effectively, crucial for non-programmers engaged in algorithmic trading.

IMPORTANCE OF DIVERSIFICATION

Diversification is a fundamental principle in portfolio management that involves allocating investments across a variety of assets to reduce overall risk exposure. By diversifying, traders can mitigate the impact of adverse market movements on their portfolios and potentially achieve more stable long-term returns.

KEY STRATEGIES FOR DIVERSIFICATION

Asset Class Diversification:

Allocate investments across multiple asset classes, including stocks, bonds, commodities, real estate, and cryptocurrencies. Each asset class behaves differently under varying market conditions, reducing correlation and enhancing portfolio stability.

Sector and Industry Diversification:

Spread investments across different sectors and industries within each asset class (e.g., technology, healthcare, consumer goods). Sector diversification mitigates risks associated with sector-specific events or economic cycles impacting individual industries.

Geographic Diversification:

Invest in assets across diverse geographic regions and markets (e.g., domestic, international, emerging markets). Geographic diversification reduces exposure to country-specific risks, political instability, and currency fluctuations.

Risk Management Integration:

Integrate risk management techniques, such as position sizing, stop-loss orders, and portfolio rebalancing, into diversified portfolios to maintain risk-adjusted returns and adapt to changing market conditions.

PORTFOLIO MANAGEMENT BEST PRACTICES

Strategic Asset Allocation:

Define a Plan: Develop a strategic asset allocation plan based on your risk tolerance, investment goals, and time horizon. This involves distributing capital across various asset classes—such as stocks, bonds, commodities, and real estate—to align with your long-term objectives.

Periodic Rebalancing: Periodically rebalance your portfolio to maintain your desired asset allocation. This helps in adjusting the portfolio in response to market changes, ensuring that it stays aligned with your risk tolerance and investment strategy.

Rebalancing Strategies:

Regular Review: Conduct regular reviews of your portfolio to check if the asset allocations have deviated from your strategic targets. Market fluctuations can cause certain assets to overperform or underperform, leading to an imbalance.

Restore Proportions: When rebalancing, buy or sell assets to restore the desired proportions. This process helps mitigate portfolio drift, maintain risk-return characteristics, and capitalize on investment opportunities.

Performance Monitoring and Evaluation:

Track Performance: Continuously monitor the performance of your portfolio, including the overall asset allocation and the performance of individual assets. This helps you assess the effectiveness of your investment strategy.

Use Tools and Benchmarks: Utilize performance analysis tools and benchmarks to track your progress towards financial goals. These tools can help identify areas for improvement, allowing for informed decisions on portfolio adjustments.

Identify Opportunities: Regular evaluation of your portfolio's performance can reveal new investment opportunities and highlight underperforming assets that may need to be replaced or rebalanced.

By implementing these best practices, you can effectively manage your investment portfolio, ensuring it remains diversified, balanced, and aligned with your financial goals.

IMPLEMENTATION IN ALGORITHMIC TRADING

Non-programmers can implement diversification strategies in algorithmic trading by selecting diversified asset classes, using multi-asset trading platforms, and incorporating risk management principles into trading strategies.

By diversifying their portfolios and managing them effectively, traders can enhance portfolio resilience, optimize risk-adjusted returns, and achieve long-term financial objectives in algorithmic trading operations.

Strategies for diversification and portfolio management are essential for non-programmers engaging in algorithmic trading to mitigate risk, enhance portfolio stability, and achieve sustainable long-term returns.

By adopting diversified strategies and adhering to best practices in portfolio management, non-programmers can navigate market uncertainties, capitalize on investment opportunities, and foster resilience in their algorithmic trading endeavors.

PART: 7: DEPLOYING AND MONITORING ALGORITHMS

CHAPTER 20: HOW TO DEPLOY YOUR ALGORITHMIC STRATEGIES IN LIVE MARKETS

Deploying strategies effectively requires careful planning, testing, and implementation to ensure optimal performance and adherence to trading objectives. In this chapter, we explore practical steps and considerations for non-programmers to successfully deploy their algorithmic trading strategies in live market environments.

PREPARATION AND PRE-DEPLOYMENT CHECKLIST

1. FINALIZE STRATEGY DEVELOPMENT:

Thorough Testing: Ensure that your algorithmic trading strategies have undergone rigorous testing, optimization, and validation through backtesting and simulated trading environments. This helps confirm that the strategies work effectively under various market conditions.

Confirm Parameters and Rules: Verify that all strategy parameters, risk management rules, and performance metrics align with your desired trading outcomes. Make necessary adjustments based on the results from testing phases to enhance strategy robustness.

2. SELECT A TRADING PLATFORM:

Platform Selection: Choose a reliable trading platform or broker that offers automated execution, real-time market data feeds, and comprehensive order management capabilities. Ensure that the platform supports the asset classes and trading instruments you intend to trade.

Verify Compatibility: Confirm that the platform is compatible with your algorithmic strategies, including any specific technical requirements or integration needs. Check for user reviews and recommendations to ensure platform reliability.

3. TECHNICAL INFRASTRUCTURE READINESS:

Stable Internet Connectivity: Ensure you have a reliable and stable internet connection to prevent disruptions in your trading operations. Consider backup connectivity options to mitigate risks of connectivity issues.

Adequate Hardware Resources: Prepare necessary hardware resources, such as a powerful computer or server, to handle the computational demands of algorithmic trading. Ensure that your hardware setup can support continuous operation and execution of trading strategies.

Backup Systems: Implement backup systems, including power backups and redundant hardware setups, to ensure uninterrupted trading operations. Regularly test these backups to confirm their effectiveness in case of primary system failures.

By completing this comprehensive preparation and pre-deployment checklist, you can ensure that your algorithmic trading operations are well-prepared, minimizing risks and enhancing the likelihood of successful strategy implementation.

DEPLOYMENT PROCESS

1. STRATEGY CONFIGURATION:

Set Up in Platform: Configure your algorithmic trading

strategies within the chosen trading platform or environment. This involves inputting all necessary strategy parameters, such as entry and exit criteria, position sizing rules, and risk management settings, to enable automated trading decisions.

Parameter Verification: Double-check that all parameters and settings are correctly inputted to avoid errors that could impact strategy execution. Ensure that the configured strategies align precisely with your pre-defined trading plans.

2. TESTING IN LIVE MARKET CONDITIONS:

Initial Live Testing: Begin with a phase of live testing or paper trading to evaluate the strategy's performance in real-time market conditions without risking actual capital. This allows you to monitor the strategy's execution accuracy, order fills, and overall behavior in a live market environment.

Observation and Adjustment: During this phase, closely observe the strategy's behavior, looking for any discrepancies or issues that may arise. Identify any necessary adjustments to improve accuracy and effectiveness before committing significant capital.

3. MONITORING AND PERFORMANCE EVALUATION:

Real-Time Monitoring: Continuously monitor the live trading performance of your strategies, focusing on trade execution, adherence to predefined risk parameters, and overall strategy outcomes. Utilize the platform's monitoring tools to track real-time data and performance metrics.

Performance Metrics Analysis: Regularly evaluate performance metrics, including profitability, drawdowns, Sharpe ratio, and other risk-adjusted return measures. Analyze these metrics to assess the strategy's effectiveness and ensure it meets your financial goals.

4. ADAPTATION AND OPTIMIZATION:

Continuous Monitoring: Keep a close watch on strategy performance and evolving market dynamics. Stay alert to any changes that may necessitate adjustments to your trading strategies.

Implement Adjustments: Based on performance analysis and market insights, make necessary adjustments to strategy parameters. This could include refining entry and exit criteria, modifying risk management rules, or optimizing position sizing.

Iterative Improvement: Adopt an iterative approach to continually improve and optimize your strategies. Regularly review strategy outcomes, implement refinements, and validate these changes through ongoing performance analysis and additional backtesting if needed.

By following these steps, you can effectively deploy your algorithmic trading strategies, ensuring they are well-configured, thoroughly tested, and continuously optimized for optimal performance in live market conditions.

RISK MANAGEMENT DURING LIVE DEPLOYMENT

Implement Stop-loss Orders: Set up stop-loss orders and other risk management measures to limit potential losses and protect trading capital during volatile market conditions.

Real-time Monitoring: Maintain vigilance over live trading activities, monitor market movements, and promptly address any anomalies or deviations from expected strategy behavior.

Deploying algorithmic trading strategies in live markets requires meticulous planning, rigorous testing, and continuous monitoring to achieve desired trading outcomes effectively.

By following best practices and leveraging advanced trading tools, non-programmers can navigate market complexities, optimize strategy performance, and capitalize on trading opportunities in algorithmic trading operations.

CHAPTER 21: TIPS FOR MONITORING PERFORMANCE AND MAKING ADJUSTMENTS

Continuous performance monitoring and proactive adjustment are crucial for maintaining strategy effectiveness, optimizing profitability, and adapting to evolving market conditions. In this chapter, we explore effective strategies and tips for non-programmers to monitor the performance of their algorithmic trading strategies and make necessary adjustments to enhance trading outcomes.

IMPORTANCE OF PERFORMANCE MONITORING

Monitoring the performance of algorithmic trading strategies allows traders to assess strategy effectiveness, track trading outcomes, and identify areas for improvement. By analyzing performance metrics and market behavior, traders can make informed decisions and adjust strategies to align with trading objectives.

Key Tips for Performance Monitoring

1. ESTABLISH PERFORMANCE BENCHMARKS:

Define Clear Benchmarks: Identify and define clear performance benchmarks and metrics to measure the success of your trading strategy. Key metrics might include profitability ratios, Sharpe ratio, maximum drawdown, win-loss ratios, and other risk-adjusted return measures.

Compare to Industry Standards: Regularly compare your strategy's performance against industry standards or competitive benchmarks to gauge its relative success and ensure it meets or exceeds market norms.

2. UTILIZE REAL-TIME MONITORING TOOLS:

Live Data Feeds: Employ trading platforms that offer live data feeds to track market movements and the real-time performance of your strategy. Access to up-to-the-minute data is crucial for timely decision-making.

Performance Dashboards: Use performance dashboards and visual analytics tools to monitor key performance indicators (KPIs). These tools help visualize performance trends, execution accuracy, and adherence to strategy parameters.

Alerts and Notifications: Set up alerts and notifications for significant market events or deviations in strategy performance. This ensures you can respond quickly to changing market conditions or strategy issues.

3. CONDUCT REGULAR PERFORMANCE REVIEWS:

Scheduled Reviews: Schedule regular performance reviews to systematically evaluate the outcomes of your trading strategy. This could be weekly, monthly, or quarterly, depending on your trading frequency and objectives.

Post-Trade Analysis: Perform detailed post-trade analysis to understand the factors contributing to each trade's success or failure. Look for patterns or trends in the trading results that can inform future strategy adjustments.

Risk Management Adherence: Validate that your trading strategy adheres to predefined risk management rules. Ensure stop-loss orders, position sizing rules, and other risk parameters are being correctly implemented and followed.

4. APPLY QUANTITATIVE ANALYSIS TECHNIQUES:

Statistical Methods: Use statistical methods to analyze historical performance data. Techniques such as mean-variance analysis can help you understand the risk-return profile of your strategy.

Regression Analysis: Apply regression analysis to identify relationships between different market variables and your strategy's performance. This can help isolate factors that significantly impact your trading outcomes.

Monte Carlo Simulations: Conduct Monte Carlo simulations to forecast potential future performance under various market scenarios. This technique can help you assess the robustness and resilience of your strategy.

Optimization Models: Develop and use optimization models to fine-tune strategy parameters. Techniques like genetic algorithms or gradient descent can be employed to find the optimal set of parameters for maximizing returns and minimizing risks.

By implementing these key tips, you can enhance your performance monitoring process, ensuring your algorithmic trading strategies remain effective, responsive, and aligned with your financial goals.

STRATEGIES FOR MAKING ADJUSTMENTS

1. DATA-DRIVEN DECISION-MAKING:

Empirical Insights: Base your strategy adjustments on empirical data insights derived from detailed performance analysis, backtesting results, and continuous market observations. This helps in making informed decisions that enhance the overall effectiveness and profitability of your trading strategy.

Refining Parameters: Use the data collected to refine strategy parameters, optimize trading rules, and identify areas for improvement. For example, if backtesting reveals that a certain entry signal consistently leads to losses, you can adjust or eliminate that signal.

Performance Metrics: Regularly review key performance metrics such as total return, Sharpe ratio, maximum drawdown, and win-loss ratios to understand the impact of different parameters and make data-driven adjustments.

2. ITERATIVE OPTIMIZATION CYCLES:

Systematic Testing: Implement iterative optimization cycles to systematically test and validate adjustments made to your algorithmic trading strategies. This involves making incremental changes, running backtests, and evaluating the results before making further modifications.

Real-time Feedback: Continuously evaluate the impact of adjustments on strategy performance using real-time feedback. This helps ensure that changes lead to the desired improvements in profitability and risk management.

A/B Testing: Consider using A/B testing methods to compare different strategy configurations. This can help you determine which adjustments yield the best performance under varying market conditions.

3. ADAPTABILITY TO MARKET CONDITIONS:

Market Dynamics: Stay responsive to changing market conditions, economic events, and levels of volatility. Adjust your strategy settings, such as entry and exit points, based on current market trends and forecasts.

Volatility Adjustments: During periods of high volatility, consider tightening risk management measures, such as reducing position sizes or setting more conservative stop-loss levels. Conversely, in stable markets, you might loosen these parameters to take advantage of consistent trends.

Economic Indicators: Monitor key economic indicators and news events that could impact market conditions. For example, during major economic announcements, you might want to pause trading or switch to a more conservative strategy to mitigate potential risks.

4. RISK MANAGEMENT INTEGRATION:

Stop-loss Orders: Ensure robust risk management practices are integrated into your adjustment processes. Use stop-loss orders to automatically exit positions that move against you, thus limiting potential losses.

Position Sizing Rules: Adjust position sizes based on risk exposure and current market conditions. For example, reduce position sizes during volatile periods to protect capital and increase them during stable periods to maximize gains.

Portfolio Rebalancing: Regularly rebalance your portfolio to maintain your desired asset allocation and risk levels. This can involve selling overperforming assets to lock in profits and buying underperforming assets to capitalize on potential recovery.

Scenario Analysis: Conduct scenario analysis to understand how potential adjustments could impact your overall risk profile and portfolio performance. This helps in planning for worst-case scenarios and ensuring your strategy remains resilient.

By employing these strategies, you can effectively make data-driven adjustments to your algorithmic trading strategies, ensuring they remain optimized, adaptable, and aligned with your financial goals while maintaining robust risk management practices.

CONTINUOUS IMPROVEMENT AND LEARNING

Educational Resources: Access educational resources, seminars, and industry publications to stay informed about latest trends, trading techniques, and regulatory developments impacting algorithmic trading strategies.

Community Engagement: Participate in online forums, trading communities, and peer discussions to exchange insights, share best practices, and collaborate with fellow traders in refining algorithmic trading strategies.

Monitoring performance and making timely adjustments are essential practices for non-programmers engaging in algorithmic trading to optimize strategy performance, mitigate risks, and achieve sustainable trading success.

By embracing continuous improvement and leveraging advanced trading tools, non-programmers can enhance trading discipline, capitalize on market opportunities, and navigate complexities in algorithmic trading operations effectively.

CHAPTER 22: UNDERSTANDING TRANSACTION COSTS AND THEIR IMPACT ON PROFITABILITY.

Understanding transaction costs is crucial for non-programmers to optimize trading strategies, manage expenses, and enhance overall trading performance in dynamic market environments. In this chapter, we delve into the significance of transaction costs in algorithmic trading and how they influence profitability.

IMPORTANCE OF TRANSACTION COSTS

Transaction costs refer to fees and expenses incurred when executing trades in financial markets. These costs include brokerage commissions, exchange fees, bid-ask spreads, slippage, and market impact costs, which collectively impact trading profitability and investment returns.

TYPES OF TRANSACTION COSTS

1. BROKERAGE COMMISSIONS:

Fees charged by brokerage firms for executing trades on behalf of traders. These fees can vary significantly depending on the brokerage firm, the volume of trades, the asset class being traded, and the level of service provided by the brokerage. Brokerage commissions can take several forms, including:

Flat-Rate Commissions: A fixed fee per trade, regardless of the trade size. For example, a broker might charge $10 per trade.

Percentage-Based Commissions: A commission calculated as a percentage of the trade's value. For instance, a 0.5% commission on a $10,000 trade would result in a $50 fee.

Tiered Commissions: Variable fees based on trade volume or account type, where higher trading volumes or specific account holders receive lower commission rates.

Per-Share Commissions: Fees calculated based on the number of shares traded, such as $0.01 per share. This model is often used for high-volume traders.

2. BID-ASK SPREADS:

The bid-ask spread is the difference between the highest price a buyer is willing to pay (bid) for an asset and the lowest price a seller is willing to accept (ask). This spread represents the cost of liquidity and is a critical factor in the execution price of trades.

Example: If the bid price for a stock is $50 and the ask price is $50.10, the bid-ask spread is $0.10. This spread can be larger in less liquid markets or during periods of high volatility, increasing the cost of executing a trade.

3. MARKET IMPACT COSTS:

Market impact costs refer to the effect that large trade orders can have on market prices. When a significant trade is placed, it can shift the market price due to the increased demand or supply, potentially leading to less favorable execution prices.

Example: If a trader attempts to buy a large number of shares in a relatively illiquid stock, the price may rise as the order is filled, resulting in higher costs for the entire order. Similarly, selling a large volume may drive the price down.

4. SLIPPAGE:

Slippage occurs when there is a difference between the expected execution price and the actual execution price of a trade. This can happen due to market fluctuations, order size, and the speed of execution, particularly in volatile or fast-moving markets.

Example: A trader places an order to buy a stock at $100, but by the time the order is executed, the price has risen to $100.50. The $0.50 difference is slippage. Slippage can be more pronounced in markets with low liquidity or high volatility.

MANAGING TRANSACTION COSTS

To minimize the impact of these transaction costs on trading performance, consider the following strategies:

Choosing Low-Cost Brokers: Select brokers with competitive commission structures, especially those offering lower rates for high-volume trading.

Trading in Liquid Markets: Focus on assets with narrow bid-ask spreads to reduce the cost of liquidity. This often involves trading more popular or heavily traded assets.

Order Execution Strategies: Use limit orders to control the execution price and minimize slippage, especially in volatile markets. Employing algorithmic trading strategies designed to minimize market impact can also help.

Regular Cost Analysis: Continuously monitor and analyze transaction costs as part of your overall trading strategy to identify areas where costs can be reduced or better managed.

By understanding and managing these types of transaction costs, traders can enhance the efficiency and profitability of their algorithmic trading strategies.

CALCULATING AND MANAGING TRANSACTION COSTS

1. COST ANALYSIS TOOLS:

Utilize transaction cost analysis (TCA) tools and software platforms to quantify and analyze transaction costs associated with algorithmic trading strategies. TCA tools provide detailed insights into various cost components, including brokerage commissions, bid-ask spreads, and market impact costs. They help traders measure execution quality by comparing actual execution prices with expected prices, assess price impact by analyzing how large orders affect market prices, and optimize trading efficiency by identifying opportunities to reduce costs and improve trade execution.

2. OPTIMIZATION STRATEGIES:

Implement optimization strategies to minimize transaction costs while maximizing trade profitability. These strategies include:

Reducing Trade Frequency: Limit the number of trades to avoid excessive transaction costs. Focus on higher-quality trades with better risk-reward ratios.

Optimizing Order Sizes: Break large orders into smaller parts to minimize market impact and slippage. Use algorithms designed for optimal order execution, such as VWAP (Volume Weighted Average Price) or TWAP (Time Weighted Average Price).

Selecting Liquidity Providers: Choose brokers and trading venues that offer competitive pricing, high liquidity, and low transaction costs. Compare the execution services of different liquidity providers to ensure cost-effective trading.

3. BENCHMARKING AND COMPARISON:

Benchmark transaction costs against industry standards, competitive brokerage rates, and alternative trading venues. Conduct regular reviews to compare:

Execution Quality: Evaluate how closely trade execution prices match expected prices and analyze any deviations.

Fee Structures: Compare commission rates, bid-ask spreads, and other fees across different brokers and trading platforms.

Trading Conditions: Assess the impact of market conditions on transaction costs, such as volatility, liquidity, and trading volume. Identify brokers or platforms that perform well under various market conditions.

By continuously monitoring and managing transaction costs through these strategies, traders can enhance the overall profitability and efficiency of their algorithmic trading operations.

IMPACT ON PROFITABILITY

Profitability Metrics:

Evaluate profitability metrics, such as net profit margins, return on investment (ROI), and risk-adjusted returns, considering transaction costs. Account for total trading expenses to assess true profitability and performance sustainability.

Risk Management Considerations:

Integrate transaction costs into risk management strategies and portfolio optimization processes. Consider cost-efficiency measures, liquidity constraints, and market conditions when adjusting trading parameters and risk exposures.

Understanding transaction costs and their impact on profitability is essential for non-programmers engaged in algorithmic trading to optimize trading strategies, manage expenses, and achieve sustainable investment returns.

By leveraging transaction cost analysis tools, implementing cost-effective trading strategies, and adhering to regulatory compliance standards, non-programmers can mitigate costs, enhance trading efficiency, and navigate complexities in algorithmic trading operations effectively.

PART: 8: PRACTICAL CONSIDERATIONS AND PITFALLS

CHAPTER 23: COMMON CHALLENGES FACED BY NON-PROGRAMMERS IN ALGORITHMIC TRADING.

In this chapter, we explore the common challenges encountered by non-programmers who are engaged in algorithmic trading. Understanding these challenges is crucial for developing effective strategies, overcoming obstacles, and achieving success in algorithmic trading endeavors.

COMPLEXITY OF TECHNOLOGY AND TOOLS

Technical Proficiency: Non-programmers may face challenges in understanding and utilizing complex trading platforms, software tools, and algorithmic trading systems requiring technical expertise.

Programming Skills: Lack of programming knowledge and coding skills can hinder non-programmers from developing or customizing algorithmic trading strategies independently.

STRATEGY DEVELOPMENT AND IMPLEMENTATION

1. STRATEGY DESIGN:

Complexity of Algorithmic Strategies: Non-programmers may find it challenging to design effective algorithmic trading strategies due to the inherent complexity of defining clear entry and exit rules, risk management protocols, and integration with market conditions. Without a programming background, translating trading ideas into executable algorithms can be difficult.

Entry/Exit Rules: Creating precise rules for entering and exiting trades requires an understanding of technical indicators, market patterns, and statistical models. Non-programmers might struggle with the nuances of these components and how to encode them into an algorithmic strategy.

Risk Management Protocols: Incorporating robust risk management measures such as stop-loss orders, position sizing rules, and diversification strategies into algorithmic trading systems requires a deep understanding of risk management principles and their algorithmic implementation.

2. TESTING AND OPTIMIZATION:

Backtesting Challenges: Conducting thorough backtesting involves simulating the trading strategy using historical market data to evaluate its performance. Non-programmers might face difficulties in setting up and running backtests, understanding the results, and ensuring the accuracy of the simulations. Accessing reliable historical data and using it effectively can also be challenging.

Optimization Techniques: Optimizing a trading strategy involves adjusting its parameters to improve performance metrics such as profitability, risk-adjusted returns, and drawdowns. Non-programmers may struggle with identifying which parameters to adjust, how to optimize them effectively, and avoiding overfitting (making the strategy too tailored to historical data, which can reduce its effectiveness in live markets).

Performance Metrics Validation: Validating the performance of a trading strategy requires analyzing various metrics, such as total return, Sharpe ratio, maximum drawdown, and win-loss ratio. Non-programmers may find it challenging to interpret these metrics, understand their implications, and make informed decisions based on the analysis.

SOLUTIONS FOR NON-PROGRAMMERS:

1. STRATEGY DESIGN TOOLS:

User-Friendly Platforms: Utilize trading platforms that offer user-friendly interfaces with drag-and-drop functionality for designing strategies. These platforms often come with pre-built technical indicators and templates to simplify strategy creation.

Educational Resources: Leverage educational resources, including tutorials, webinars, and community forums, provided by trading platforms to understand the basics of strategy design, technical indicators, and risk management.

2. BACKTESTING AND OPTIMIZATION TOOLS:

Integrated Backtesting: Choose platforms that offer integrated backtesting tools with easy-to-use interfaces, allowing non-programmers to run simulations and analyze results without coding.

Automated Optimization: Use platforms with automated optimization features that can adjust strategy parameters based on performance metrics. These tools help non-programmers optimize their strategies efficiently.

Data Access: Ensure access to reliable and comprehensive historical data through trading platforms or third-party data providers. This is crucial for accurate backtesting and validation.

3. PERFORMANCE METRICS AND ANALYSIS:

Visual Analytics: Utilize platforms that offer visual analytics and performance dashboards, making it easier to interpret backtest results and performance metrics through graphs and charts.

Benchmark Comparisons: Compare strategy performance against benchmarks or indices to contextualize results and understand relative performance.

Consulting Experts: Consider consulting with trading strategy experts or joining algorithmic trading communities where experienced traders can provide insights, feedback, and support in strategy development and optimization.

By leveraging these tools and resources, non-programmers can overcome the challenges associated with strategy development and implementation, enhancing their ability to participate in algorithmic trading effectively.

EDUCATION AND CONTINUOUS LEARNING

Knowledge Acquisition: Continuous learning and skill development in algorithmic trading strategies, financial markets, technical analysis, and emerging technologies influencing trading practices.

Community Support: Accessing peer networks, educational resources, mentorship programs, and online communities to exchange insights, share experiences, and seek guidance from experienced traders.

Navigating algorithmic trading as a non-programmer presents various challenges, from technical complexities and strategy development to risk management, regulatory compliance, and psychological resilience.

By addressing these challenges proactively, non-programmers

can enhance trading proficiency, optimize algorithmic strategies, and achieve sustainable success in algorithmic trading operations.

CHAPTER 24: TECHNOLOGY AND INFRASTRUCTURE REQUIREMENTS

In the realm of algorithmic trading, robust technology and infrastructure are fundamental to the successful execution of automated strategies. This chapter explores the critical elements and considerations essential for setting up and maintaining the necessary technological framework.

In today's financial markets, algorithmic trading relies heavily on advanced technology to execute trades swiftly and efficiently. Non-programmers entering this domain need a clear understanding of the technological requirements and infrastructure to support their trading strategies effectively.

KEY COMPONENTS OF TECHNOLOGY AND INFRASTRUCTURE

1. HARDWARE REQUIREMENTS:

Algorithmic trading places high demands on hardware capabilities due to the need for rapid data processing and trade execution:

Computing Power: For optimal performance in algorithmic trading, it's essential to use high-performance computers or servers. These should be equipped with multicore processors and ample RAM to swiftly handle complex algorithms and data-intensive calculations. A recommended minimum requirement includes multicore processors with high clock speeds and at least 16 GB of RAM to ensure smooth execution of trading algorithms and efficient processing of real-time market data.

Redundancy: Implementation of backup systems, redundant power supplies, and mirrored data storage to ensure continuity of operations and minimize downtime in case of hardware failures.

Scalability: Ability to scale hardware resources seamlessly as trading volumes grow or when implementing more sophisticated trading strategies. Scalability ensures that the infrastructure can handle increased computational loads without performance degradation.

2. SOFTWARE AND PLATFORMS:

Choosing the right software and trading platforms is critical for non-programmers to effectively manage algorithmic trading strategies:

Algorithmic Trading Platforms: Opt for platforms tailored for automated trading, equipped with features like algorithm development environments, robust backtesting capabilities, real-time data feeds, and comprehensive order management systems.

Technical Analysis Tools: Integrate tools that support thorough backtesting, strategy optimization, and real-time data analysis. These include charting software, statistical analysis packages, and algorithmic libraries designed to simplify strategy development and testing.

User Interface: Select platforms with intuitive interfaces that facilitate easy strategy configuration, monitoring, and adjustment without the need for extensive programming skills. User-friendly interfaces enable seamless interaction, allowing traders to modify parameters and monitor strategy performance in real time.

Minimum Recommended Operating System: Ensure compatibility with modern operating systems such as Windows 10 or macOS Catalina (version 10.15) to leverage the latest software updates, security patches, and compatibility with trading platform requirements.

3. INTERNET CONNECTIVITY:

Having reliable and high-speed internet connectivity is crucial for efficient order execution and timely data transmission:

Latency: Minimize latency, which is the delay in network response time, to ensure trade orders are executed promptly at desired prices. Low latency helps prevent slippage and ensures accurate execution of trading strategies, particularly in volatile market conditions.

Backup Connectivity: Implement redundant internet connections or failover mechanisms to maintain uninterrupted connectivity during network outages or disruptions. Backup connectivity safeguards against downtime, ensuring continuous operation of trading systems and avoiding missed trading opportunities due to internet interruptions.

Minimum Recommended Internet Speed: Aim for a minimum internet speed of at least 25 Mbps for stable and efficient data transmission, ensuring optimal performance when accessing real-time market data and executing trades.

4. DATA FEEDS AND APIS:

Access to accurate and comprehensive market data is essential for making informed trading decisions:

Market Data Feeds: Integration of real-time data feeds providing up-to-date price quotes, market depth information, and historical data. Reliable market data feeds enable traders to analyze market trends, identify trading opportunities, and execute timely trades.

API Integration: Utilization of application programming interfaces (APIs) for seamless integration with external data sources, order execution platforms, and trading algorithms. APIs facilitate data retrieval, automate trade execution, and support integration with third-party services or proprietary trading systems.

IMPLEMENTATION CONSIDERATIONS

1. TESTING AND SIMULATION:

Before deploying algorithmic trading strategies in live markets, rigorous testing and simulation are essential:

Backtesting: Conduct comprehensive backtesting using historical market data to assess strategy performance across various market conditions. Backtesting helps validate trading rules, optimize parameters, and estimate potential risks and returns.

Forward Testing: Perform forward testing or paper trading to simulate strategy performance in real-time market conditions without risking actual capital. This stage allows traders to observe how strategies perform in live environments and make necessary adjustments before executing real trades.

Scenario Analysis: Conduct scenario-based testing to evaluate strategy resilience under different economic scenarios, market volatilities, and geopolitical events. Scenario analysis helps anticipate potential outcomes and refine risk management protocols accordingly.

2. SECURITY MEASURES:

Ensuring robust cybersecurity measures is crucial for individual traders to protect sensitive trading data and maintain operational integrity:

Data Encryption: Implement strong encryption protocols to secure data transmission and storage, safeguarding confidential trading information from unauthorized access or cyber threats.

Access Control: Utilize multi-factor authentication (MFA) and role-based access controls (RBAC) to restrict access to trading platforms and sensitive data, ensuring that only authorized personnel can access critical information.

Monitoring and Auditing: Regularly monitor system activities, audit logs, and network traffic for any signs of unusual behavior or security breaches. Implement intrusion detection systems (IDS) and establish security incident response plans to swiftly address and mitigate potential security incidents. These measures help in maintaining the integrity and security of trading operations, protecting against data breaches and unauthorized access.

3. COMPLIANCE AND REGULATIONS:

For individual traders, adherence to regulatory requirements is essential to mitigate legal risks and uphold ethical trading practices:

Data Privacy: Ensure compliance with data privacy regulations such as GDPR (General Data Protection Regulation) or CCPA (California Consumer Privacy Act) when handling personal or client data. Implement measures to protect sensitive information and uphold privacy rights.

Algorithmic Trading Regulations: Understand and comply with regulatory guidelines specific to algorithmic trading practices. This includes adherence to rules concerning market manipulation, fair trading practices, and reporting obligations to regulatory bodies.

Documentation and Reporting: Maintain accurate and comprehensive documentation of trading strategies, algorithms, and transaction records. Ensure timely and transparent reporting to regulatory authorities regarding trading activities and performance metrics, demonstrating compliance with regulatory standards. These practices help individual traders navigate regulatory complexities and uphold integrity in their trading operations.

By addressing these implementation considerations, traders can enhance the reliability, security, and compliance of their algorithmic trading operations. Thorough testing and simulation mitigate operational risks, robust cybersecurity measures protect sensitive data, and adherence to regulatory requirements fosters trust and transparency in trading practices.

Navigating the technological landscape of algorithmic trading requires careful consideration of hardware, software, connectivity, and data requirements. You can leverage advanced tools and platforms to streamline strategy implementation and enhance trading effectiveness in dynamic market environments.

CHAPTER 25: STRATEGIES FOR DEALING WITH MARKET VOLATILITY AND UNEXPECTED EVENTS.

Addressing volatility challenges requires adaptive strategies, risk management protocols, and proactive measures to mitigate potential risks and optimize trading outcomes. In this chapter, we explore effective strategies and considerations to manage market volatility and navigate unexpected events in algorithmic trading.

UNDERSTANDING MARKET VOLATILITY

Market volatility refers to the degree of variation and fluctuations in asset prices over time. It reflects the speed and extent of price changes in financial markets, influenced by various factors such as economic indicators, geopolitical events, and investor sentiment. Higher volatility indicates greater uncertainty and risk in asset pricing, while lower volatility suggests more stable price movements.

IMPACT ON TRADING STRATEGIES:

Market volatility significantly impacts algorithmic trading strategies by affecting trade execution, price movements, and overall risk exposure. In volatile markets, prices can change rapidly, leading to increased price slippage and execution challenges. Algorithmic strategies may experience higher transaction costs and heightened risk of stop-loss triggers due to sudden price swings. Traders must adapt strategies to handle volatility effectively, considering market dynamics and risk management protocols.

STRATEGIES FOR MANAGING MARKET VOLATILITY

1. DIVERSIFICATION AND ASSET ALLOCATION:

Diversifying investments across different asset classes, sectors, and geographic regions is a fundamental strategy to mitigate the impact of market volatility. By spreading risk exposure, traders can reduce the correlation between assets and potentially offset losses in one area with gains in another. Diversification enhances portfolio resilience and helps maintain stable returns despite fluctuations in specific markets or sectors.

2. DYNAMIC RISK MANAGEMENT:

Implementing dynamic risk management techniques is crucial during volatile market phases. This includes using stop-loss orders to limit potential losses by automatically selling a security when it reaches a predetermined price level. Adjusting position sizes based on volatility levels helps control risk exposure relative to market conditions. Regular portfolio rebalancing ensures that asset allocations remain aligned with long-term investment objectives, adapting to changing market volatility and minimizing downside risk.

3 ADAPTIVE TRADING STRATEGIES:

Developing adaptive trading strategies is essential for navigating fluctuating market conditions effectively. Adaptive strategies incorporate flexibility to adjust trading parameters, algorithmic rules, and decision-making criteria in response to evolving volatility levels and unexpected events. Utilizing real-time data analytics enables traders to capture market opportunities, optimize trade execution, and enhance strategy performance amidst changing market dynamics.

By continuously refining algorithms and monitoring market signals, traders can optimize risk-adjusted returns and maintain competitiveness in volatile environments.

RISK MITIGATION TECHNIQUES

1. LEVERAGE HEDGING INSTRUMENTS:

Hedging is a fundamental risk management strategy used to offset potential losses from adverse market movements. Traders can employ various hedging instruments such as options, futures contracts, and derivatives. For instance, buying put options can protect against downside risk in stock holdings, while futures contracts allow for locking in future prices to hedge against price fluctuations in commodities. By using hedging strategies, traders can mitigate volatility risks, protect portfolio value, and enhance overall risk-adjusted returns.

SCENARIO ANALYSIS AND STRESS TESTING:

Scenario analysis and stress testing are proactive risk management practices essential for assessing strategy resilience under different market conditions, especially during periods of heightened volatility. Traders simulate hypothetical scenarios, such as market crashes or economic downturns, to evaluate the performance of their trading strategies. Stress testing helps identify potential weaknesses, assess liquidity needs, and refine risk mitigation strategies to better withstand adverse market events. By preparing for worst-case scenarios through rigorous testing, traders can enhance their preparedness and decision-making capabilities during turbulent market conditions.

OPERATIONAL PREPAREDNESS

1. CONTINGENCY PLANNING:

Contingency planning involves developing comprehensive protocols and procedures to ensure operational continuity and minimize disruptions in algorithmic trading operations. Traders should establish contingency plans for system failures, technical disruptions, and unexpected events that may impact trading activities. This includes deploying backup systems, redundant data centers, and alternative communication channels to maintain connectivity and functionality during emergencies. Clear escalation procedures and crisis management protocols enable swift responses to mitigate potential losses and uphold trading integrity.

2. REAL-TIME MONITORING AND SURVEILLANCE:

Implementing robust real-time monitoring tools and market surveillance systems is critical for detecting and responding to sudden changes in market volatility and abnormal trading patterns. Automated alerts and monitoring systems enable traders to monitor key metrics, such as price movements, trading volumes, and volatility spikes, in real time.

By proactively identifying unusual market behavior or potential risks, traders can take immediate corrective actions, such as adjusting trading strategies, activating stop-loss orders, or suspending trading activities to protect capital and minimize adverse impacts from volatile market conditions.

PSYCHOLOGICAL RESILIENCE AND DECISION-MAKING

1. EMOTIONAL DISCIPLINE:

Emotional discipline is crucial for traders to maintain

composure and make rational decisions amidst the inherent uncertainty and emotional highs and lows of financial markets. It involves controlling emotions such as fear, greed, and impatience that can lead to impulsive trading decisions. Traders with emotional discipline are better equipped to stick to their trading plans, adhere to risk management rules, and avoid chasing losses or making irrational trades during volatile market conditions. Techniques such as mindfulness, meditation, and cognitive behavioral strategies can help traders cultivate emotional resilience and maintain focus on long-term trading objectives despite short-term market fluctuations.

2. RISK ASSESSMENT AND ADAPTATION:

Effective risk assessment involves regularly evaluating one's risk tolerance, understanding potential market risks, and adapting trading strategies accordingly. Traders should continuously monitor economic trends, geopolitical developments, and market volatility to anticipate potential impacts on their portfolios.

By conducting thorough risk assessments, traders can identify vulnerabilities in their trading strategies, adjust position sizes, implement dynamic risk management techniques such as trailing stop-loss orders, and diversify investments across different asset classes.

By integrating adaptive strategies, leveraging risk mitigation techniques, and fostering psychological resilience, non-programmers can effectively navigate market.

CHAPTER 26: RESOURCES AND FURTHER READING

In this chapter, we compile a comprehensive list of resources, recommended readings, and educational materials for individuals looking to expand their knowledge and expertise in automated trading. Whether you are a beginner or an experienced trader, these resources offer valuable insights, practical guidance, and advanced strategies to enhance your understanding and proficiency in algorithmic trading.

BOOKS ON ALGORITHMIC TRADING

Algorithmic Trading: Winning Strategies and Their Rationale by Ernest P. Chan

Explore proven strategies, quantitative analysis techniques, and risk management principles for algorithmic trading success.

Quantitative Trading: Algorithms, Analytics, Data, Models, Optimization by Ernie Chan

Delve into quantitative trading methodologies, financial modeling, and optimization techniques using real-world examples and practical applications.

Algorithmic Trading and DMA: An Introduction to Direct Access Trading Strategies by Barry Johnson

Gain insights into direct market access (DMA), algorithmic

trading strategies, execution algorithms, and technological innovations shaping modern trading practices.

ONLINE COURSES AND TUTORIALS

Coursera - Algorithmic Trading Courses

Enroll in courses covering algorithmic trading fundamentals, quantitative finance, machine learning applications in trading, and portfolio management strategies.

Udemy - Algorithmic Trading Bootcamps

Access hands-on training, coding tutorials, and practical workshops on algorithmic trading strategies, programming languages (Python, R), and algorithm development.

edX - Financial Markets and Algorithmic Trading Courses

Explore courses on financial markets, trading algorithms, derivatives pricing, and risk management offered by leading universities and industry experts.

RESEARCH PAPERS AND JOURNALS

Journal of Finance

Access academic research papers, empirical studies, and theoretical frameworks on financial markets, algorithmic trading strategies, and market microstructure.

Quantitative Finance

Stay updated with quantitative finance research, mathematical modeling techniques, algorithmic trading innovations, and computational finance advancements.

ONLINE PLATFORMS AND COMMUNITIES

Quantopian

Join an online platform offering algorithmic trading simulations, educational resources, community forums, and access to algorithm libraries for quantitative analysis.

Kaggle

Participate in data science competitions, machine learning challenges, and algorithmic trading datasets to practice data analysis, model development, and predictive modeling.

INDUSTRY CONFERENCES AND WEBINARS

TradeTech

Attend industry conferences, seminars, and webinars on algorithmic trading, market technologies, regulatory developments, and trading strategies hosted by leading financial institutions and technology providers.

QuantCon

Engage in quantitative finance conferences, networking events, and workshops focusing on algorithmic trading innovations, machine learning applications, and investment strategies.

REGULATORY AND COMPLIANCE RESOURCES

Securities and Exchange Commission (SEC)

Access regulatory guidelines, enforcement actions, and compliance updates related to algorithmic trading practices, market surveillance, and investor protection.

Financial Industry Regulatory Authority (FINRA)

Stay informed about regulatory compliance requirements, trading rules, and industry standards governing automated trading activities in financial markets.

The resources and further reading recommendations provided in this chapter serve as valuable tools for individuals interested in deepening their understanding and expertise in automated trading.

Whether you are exploring algorithmic trading strategies, learning programming languages, or navigating regulatory complexities, these resources offer diverse perspectives, practical insights, and educational opportunities to enhance your skills and proficiency in algorithmic trading.

By leveraging these resources effectively, staying updated with industry trends, and continuously learning from reputable sources, you can optimize trading strategies, mitigate risks, and achieve sustainable success in algorithmic trading operations.

CONCLUSION AND NEXT STEPS

In this book, Algorithmic Trading 101: A Practical Introduction to Automated Market Trading for Non-Programmers, we have explored the fundamentals, strategies, and practical applications of algorithmic trading tailored for individuals without extensive programming experience. From understanding algorithmic trading basics to exploring advanced topics like machine learning, each chapter has provided valuable insights and actionable strategies to empower your journey into automated trading.

KEY TAKEAWAYS

Understanding Algorithmic Trading: We started by defining algorithmic trading and exploring its benefits, risks, and the role it plays in modern financial markets.

Practical Applications: You learned about different financial instruments, market orders, and trading strategies that can be implemented without extensive programming knowledge.

Tools and Platforms: We discussed how to choose, set up, and leverage algorithmic trading platforms and services that support automated trading.

Resources and Further Learning: Finally, we provided a comprehensive list of resources, recommended readings, and educational materials to support your continued learning and development in automated trading.

NEXT STEPS

As you conclude this book, consider the following next steps to further enhance your skills and proficiency in algorithmic trading:

Continuous Learning: Stay updated with industry trends, technological advancements, and regulatory changes through online courses, books, and industry conferences.

Practice and Experimentation: Apply theoretical knowledge by experimenting with algorithmic trading simulations, coding exercises, and real-time market data analysis.

Network and Collaborate: Engage with like-minded professionals, join online communities, and participate in trading competitions to exchange ideas and gain practical insights.

Refine Strategies: Continuously evaluate and refine your trading strategies based on performance metrics, backtesting results, and market feedback to optimize trading outcomes.

Stay Informed: Regularly monitor financial news, market analyses, and economic indicators to make informed trading decisions and adapt strategies to changing market conditions.

Algorithmic trading offers unprecedented opportunities for individuals to automate trading processes, optimize decision-making, and capitalize on market efficiencies. Whether you are a novice trader or an experienced investor, the principles and strategies discussed in this book provide a solid foundation for navigating the complexities of automated market trading.

By embracing learning, leveraging technology, and maintaining a disciplined approach, you can unlock the potential of algorithmic trading to achieve your financial goals and enhance your trading proficiency. Success in algorithmic trading requires continuous learning, adaptability to market dynamics, and a commitment to ethical trading practices.

Thank you for embarking on this journey with us. Wishing you success and fulfillment in your algorithmic trading endeavors!

ABOUT THE AUTHOR

Usiere Uko

Usiere Uko is a writer, speaker and business and finance coach. Aside from running other businesses, he is involved in helping entrepreneurs grow their businesses and attain their potential through a faith-based business academy and empowerment programs.

Originally trained as a mechanical engineer with extensive experience in the oil industry spanning design, construction, project management and organisational capability, his passion has been to educate people to achieve their fullest potential and live fully through acquiring skills (especially financial skills) to enable them to achieve freedom in other areas of their lives as an integrated whole.

Among the publications he has written for includes Punch (AM Business) and Daily Trust (SME Business) Newspapers, Leadership & Lifestyle and Today's Lifeline magazines.

Usiere is happily married with a lovely son and daughter.

BOOKS IN THIS SERIES
ONLINE TRADING FOR BEGINNERS

Day Trading 101: A Complete Beginner's Guide To Trading The Markets

Online Stock Trading 101: A Beginner's Guide To Profitable Trading

Forex Trading 101: A Beginner's Guide And Strategies To Profitable Currency Trading

Scalping Strategies 101: Proven Profitable Trading Tactics For Beginner Traders

Options Trading 101: A Beginner's Guide To Trading Stock Options

Futures Trading 101: A Step-By-Step Guide And Strategies For Beginner Traders

Binary Options Trading 101: A Beginner's Guide

To Smart And Profitable Trades

Crypto Trading 101: A Beginner's Guide To Profiting From Cryptocurrency

Cfd Trading 101: A Beginner's Handbook For Profitable Contracts For Difference Trading

BOOKS BY THIS AUTHOR

Practical Steps To Financial Freedom And Independence: Money Management Skills For Beginners

Before You Trade Forex: Things You Need To Know If You Desire To Start Trading Forex Profitably

Before You Invest In Cryptocurrency: A Simple Guide To Understanding The Cryptocurrency Market

101 Common Money Mistakes To Avoid: And How To Fix Them. Book 1: Expenses. Money Management, Making Your Budget Work

How To Avoid Living Under Financial Pressure: A Simple Guide To Getting Back Control Of Your Finances

Financial Independence For Employees: Making

Your Job A Stepping Stone To Exiting The Rat Race And Living Your Dreams

Managing Your Money Post Covid: Financial Management Skills For An Era Of High Inflation And Market Disruption

Retire On Your Own Terms: A Simple Guide To Financially Literate Retirement Planning

Your Ultimate Money Makeover: Manage Your Money Better, Take Control Of Your Finances And Your Life

Teaching Kids Money 101: Simple Parenting Strategies For Raising Financially Literate Kids From Toddler To Teen Years And Beyond

Uncle Ben's Money Lessons: Book I: Do You Want To Work For Money? A Vacation Story With An Adventure Into The World Of Money

Nft Investing 101: A Beginner's Guide To Collectible Digital Assets

Stock Market Investing 101: A Practical Beginners

Guide To Online And Offline Stock Trading

Investing In Etfs 101: A Beginner's Guide For Building Wealth With Exchange-Traded Funds

Day Trading 101: A Complete Beginner's Guide To Trading The Markets

Forex Trading 101: A Beginner's Guide And Strategies To Profitable Currency Trading

Options Trading 101: A Beginner's Guide To Trading Stock Options

Futures Trading 101: A Step-By-Step Guide And Strategies For Beginner Traders

www.ingramcontent.com/pod-product-compliance
Lightning Source LLC
Chambersburg PA
CBHW071920210526
45479CB00002B/493